POWER BEYOND CORONAVIRUS PANDEMIC

It shall not come near you nor shall any plague come near your dwelling

Samuel Kioko Kiema

ISBN 978-1-953223-74-6 (paperback)
ISBN 978-1-953223-73-9 (hardcover)
ISBN 978-1-953223-72-2 (digital)

Copyright © 2020 by Samuel Kioko Kiema

All rights reserved. No part of this publication may be reproduced, distributed, or transmitted in any form or by any means, including photocopying, recording, or other electronic or mechanical methods without the prior written permission of the publisher. For permission requests, solicit the publisher via the address below.

Rushmore Press LLC
1 800 460 9188
www.rushmorepress.com

Printed in the United States of America

PREFACE

The world is not only at war with a deadly coronavirus pandemic, but each of us also has a personal battle against the forces of evil.

The predominant and most urgent of all our needs right now is to come into right standing with God that we may obtain mercy and find grace to help us in this time of need. This worldwide pandemic reminds us that the return of Christ is closing in. We all need spiritual preparation as we face the final events of the Gentile age. If you seek Him, He will be found by you, but if you forsake Him, He will cast you off forever. We cannot afford to seek Him when we want. It might be too late.

Therefore, we must be *our* brother's keeper to keep spiritually strong and healthy—exhorting *one another,* and so much the more as we see the Day approaching.

ACKNOWLEDGMENTS

First, to my Lord and Savior, Jesus Christ, who has prepared and anointed me to herald His gospel. I am honored to be charged with such a responsibility. I am forever grateful for His perpetual grace upon my life so that I may make known the power of His gospel. Thank you, Lord, for delighting in the prosperity of your servant. I declare my best days are with me—speaking blessing, favor, increase, and multiplication into my tomorrow.

To my beautiful, excellent, godly wife; my intimate and covenant friend; the love of my life; and my coworker in God's purpose, Jedidah, who continues to show me the joy of life—I thank the Lord for such a perfect match for my strengths and weaknesses. The trust you have in my ability to see and hear from God causes me to walk in a deeper level of fear of the Lord. I thank you for your chaste conduct accompanied by godly fear, for sharing this work with me, and encouraging me to do all that God has assigned us. You are the most profound representation of Jesus I have ever known. Your walk of love, humility, forgiveness, gentleness, and faith challenges me daily. I thank you for being a loving mother to our three children, Faith, Susan, and Samuel Jr., whom you have helped to raise in the fear of the Lord. I thank you for believing the gift of God in me and requesting that I write this book. What a treasure and jewel you are to me. You are my world, my sunshine, my precious gift from the Father. Through you, I have obtained favor with the Lord. Thank you for trusting me to lead you into the purposes of God. My world revolves around you.

To my bishop, apostle, and prophetic friend, Bishop Clarence E. McClendon of Full Harvest International Church and of Clarence E. McClendon Ministries, who helped father me into the service of our Lord Jesus Christ to connect people to the power of God—thank you for prophesying to my destiny, preaching revelatory Rhema word, teaching, and training me how to speak God's Word to situations that speak contrary to my destiny as well as how to pray the word of God and get results, how to hear the voice of God, and how to discern and respond to issues knowing that the issue is never the matter in a situation. You helped develop the gifts of God in me. I honor you.

To my mother, Martha, who helped raise me in the fear of God amid destitution and impoverishment and believed that I would become a blessing, knowing that I was called to this and would become a blessing to others—I am blessed by your strength and your example of humility. You discerned the gift of God in me and helped to develop it. I call you blessed.

To the faithful, trustworthy covenant friend pastor Josephine Kanywele, whom the Lord has connected to my anointing as I seek to connect people to the kingdom of God and equip the saints for the work of the ministry, establishing them in the foundation of God that stands sure—thank you for encouraging my faith and strengthening me in the things of God by sowing into the anointing the *Great Commission* that prepares people to enter into the kingdom of our Lord. May the Lord give you and your children an increase more and more. I call you coworker with us in the Lord's big business.

To daughters, Faith-Kiema Phillips and Susan Kiema Adams; my son, Samuel Kioko Kiema Jr.; my sons-in-law, Seilas Phillips and Michael Adams; and my grandchildren, Solomon, Zoe, Drusilla, and Zion—I thank you for your support and maturity in letting me fulfill the great calling of my life. The Lord bless you on credit as you mature in the things of God. You are my earthly inheritance.

INTRODUCTION

We have learned from health experts through the media that COVID-19 is a contagious viral disease which was officially declared as a pandemic after it first emerged in China and rapidly spread to the rest of the globe—infecting over 2.2 million people with fatalities exceeding 150,000 by the time of writing this book. Humanity is hurting, and earthly wisdom doesn't have an answer. Medical science experts have told us through the news media that there is no cure for COVID-19. The American government has been cited inaction, but frankly speaking, the president, his administration, and the counsel around him don't have the answer. Supernatural intervention is most needed now and not later to save the situation.

But what is a pandemic and what are its implications? COVID-19 pandemic is a new disease that people aren't immune to and is spreading around the world beyond expectations. All of a sudden, the number of COVID-19 cases is increasing exponentially daily. Thousands are fighting for their lives in hospitals. The medical experts who are coming on the news media are bringing more depressing news that "In the days and weeks ahead, we expect to see the number of cases, the number of deaths, and the number of affected countries climb even higher". They have been assessing COVID-19 outbursts around the clock and are deeply concerned both by the alarming levels of spread, severity, and inaction. The assessment of the threat posed by this coronavirus pandemic has never been seen before. One of the deadliest pandemics in history was the Black Death, which killed around 200 million people in the

Late Middle Ages, and smallpox, which killed about 300 million in the 20th century. Nations are struggling with a lack of resolve because COVID-19 has yet no cure.

In the austere situations brought by COVID-19, we are not without help. Our help is in the name of the Lord. In moments like these, we need supernatural intervention, for only a miracle will settle the questions. When the world has no answer, the Word of God provides it in heavenly wisdom. James 3:17 says ". . . . the **wisdom** that is from **above** is first pure, then peaceable, gentle, willing to yield, full of mercy and good fruits, without partiality and without hypocrisy." God is omniscient—He is all-knowing and liberally gives wisdom without reproach to all who ask for it so they know how to deal with dreadful situations like the coronavirus pandemic. God will protect us from the pandemic, so we are safe; and in case the pandemic infects, God will provide a way of escape.

This book will help the readers discover the weapons they can use against mass destruction, which is also applicable to every warfare they may have—physical, psychological, material, and spiritual such as COVID-19 pandemic which is also a spiritual battle. These weapons of warfare are all by God's might to help us pull down strongholds. You must understand that when we make GOD our refuge and take the Most High our dwelling place, there will be no evil or plague that can come near our dwelling. "He becomes our refuge and fortress. Surely He delivers us from the perilous pestilence and under His wings we take refuge" (Psalm 91).

In other words, you haven't seen anything yet, so what will you do when the next trouble comes? Only in the Lord do we find a safe haven. We the righteous can use the word of God to stop his sure foundations from being destroyed. The Word of God records in 2 Samuel 22:31 that in seasons of trouble, we can find refuge in God—"As for God, His way is perfect; the word of the Lord is proven; He is a shield to all who trust in Him".

The synoptic Gospel contains various indicative signs of when the end is near. The writers warned about times when the followers of Jesus will be persecuted and brought before judges and kings. Family members will turn against one another. We have seen a lot of these prophesies fulfilled. There have been wars and natural disasters of all kinds such as earthquakes, floods, famines, droughts, storms, tsunamis—you name it. It's obvious that there is still more to come, including a strange, perplexing, tormenting virus other than COVID-19. The fall of mankind brought all manners of troubles as a consequence. All the predictions of the Bible about the end of the world leaves us with a terrifying picture of "the coming of the day of God, which will cause the burning heavens to be dissolved and the elements to be melted with fervent heat". Jesus told us in Luke 21:28, "Now when these things begin to happen, look up and lift up your heads, because your redemption draws near," and in Luke 13:18–19, "Pray that your flight may not be in winter. For in those days there will be tribulation, such as has not been since the beginning of the creation which God created until this time, nor ever shall be".

There have been so many orders and restrictive measures that have been released through our national, federal, state, and local governments relative to the gathering of people around the earth. The entire globe literally has been on lockdown. Here we are in a brand-new time and season with **fear** sweeping across the globe. News stations and social media have been acting as portals of **fear** in homes, but there is only one way to fight it with a stronger force—it's called **faith**. So right now, we have breaking news, the good news

CHAPTER 1

Breaking News

People all over the world have been asked to social distance themselves by staying at home to keep COVID-19 from spreading. However, there is one thing that continues to spread on a massive scale even when everyone is staying at home, and that is **fear**. **Fear** is the enemy's most popular weapon that he uses against humanity. Worry, anxiety, fear—all of these are designed purposely to overwhelm us with a thick shadow of darkness—controlling our every move and decision in the name of quarantining ourselves.

God records it in Ezekiel 7:6-7, "An end has come. The end has come. It has dawned for you, behold, it has come! Doom has come to you, you who dwell in the land; the time has come, a day of trouble is near, and not of rejoicing in the mountains."

In times of plagues and pestilences like COVID-19, you and I need an anchor that holds on the solid rock—that is, the Lord Jesus, as our refuge and fortress. Jesus said that these are the beginnings of sorrows and the end of an age. Jesus prophesies saying in Mark 13:7-8—"7 But when you hear of wars and rumors of wars, do not be troubled; for such things must happen, but the end is not yet. For nation will rise against nation, and kingdom against kingdom. And there will be earthquakes in various places, and there will be famines and troubles. These are the beginnings of sorrows".

in the Word of God, the gospel that promises protection over the people who live by **faith** in him despite perilous pestilences like COVID-19. This good news of God's kingdom dominion on earth overcomes every catastrophe that comes against us and provides supernatural protection to those who place their **faith** in God. The Lord Jesus said that these things and unpreceded times would come and that we now have to respond with **faith** in the Word of God for supernatural protection. The good news doesn't stop there. **Jehovah Rohi**, the Lord who is our shepherd and the bishop of our souls, is our protection. He is also **Jehovah Rapha,** the Lord our healer.

I am excited by what the spirit of God is doing in the earth and shall be doing starting right now. At the beginning of the year 2020, before the COVID-19 pandemic came to hit the globe, we were dealing with very specific matters in our ministry on the protection of the upright as recorded in the following:

> Psalm 112:4, 6–8—"⁴ Unto the upright there arises light in the darkness; He is gracious, and full of compassion, and righteous. ⁶ Surely he will never be shaken; The righteous will be in everlasting remembrance. ⁷ He will not be afraid of evil tidings; His heart is steadfast, trusting in the LORD. ⁸ His heart is established; He will not be afraid, Until he sees his desire upon his enemies."

Declaration:

1. Father, I decree light arises in the darkness for me.
2. I am gracious, compassionate, and righteous (upright—in right standing with you).
3. I am gracious, a lender, and it is well with me.
4. I conduct my affairs with justice and I am never shaken.
5. Lord, I am in right standing with you and you remember me forever.
6. I do not fear bad news because my heart is steadfast, trusting [confidently relying on and believing] in you, Lord.

Now I recognize that the Lord was preparing us to minister to you the word of God, the word of truth, and the spirit of God during these times of perilous pestilence. Now we are coming to you through this book in an unlimited fashion. We have set ourselves in a posture of prayer to get the mind of God in these fearful times because we recognize the growing concern regarding the spread of the COVID-19 pandemic. It is our conviction that in these times of great public perplexity and fear, the public ministry of the word of God and the spirit of God under his anointing is not a public health risk, but is indeed a public health service. The ministry of Jesus is a teaching, preaching, and healing ministry as articulated in Matthew 4:23 and Matthew 9:35 and following which say the same thing that "Jesus went about preaching the gospel of the kingdom teaching in synagogues, healing all manner of sickness and disease among the people".

Jesus heals the COVID-19 pandemic; therefore, there is no reason to **fear** or be **afraid**. We believe that his ministry has to continue. I am of the conviction that this great public perplexity is only going to last long based on the breaking news from the highest source, the Omniscient One. Right now, I declare and decree healing to you who are experiencing symptoms of COVID-19 and any other would-be attacks.

Declaration:

"I command you disease and sickness who have come against God's inheritance to lift and go, in Jesus' name."

In the wake of looming global crises, we are witnessing before our very eyes a day of trouble and distress; a day of devastation and desolation; a day of gloominess; and a day of clouds and thick darkness. We are in the genesis of a season of glooming plagues, pestilences, and trouble, all of which have come unexpectedly.

However, the children of God are not without recourse. The LORD preserves his anointed and answers him from his holy heaven with the saving strength of his right hand. Some *trust* in chariots and some in horses, but we will remember the name of the LORD our God to help us.

The children of God have light in their dwellings—the light and life of the gospel that **kindles in the darkness.** In seasons of desperation, the sons of God are indeed not without recourse but have a place of refuge to go for any present and future crises, including COVID-19. That place is described in the Word of God, which reminds us where to put our trust for prevention and relief from plagues in case you and I are attacked. It is only God who can stop and heal a pandemic, but we must call on the Lord like a psalmist and declare.

Declaration:

Psalm 22:11—"Father be not far from me. For trouble is near. For there is none to help, but You."

The word **prevention** means obstruction, restraint, or discontinue. In the healthcare system, we say, "prevention is better than cure"; social distancing and quarantining explains it all as God declared in Psalm 91:10, "No evil shall befall you, nor shall any plague come near your dwelling".

Declaration:

"In the name of Jesus, no evil shall befall me, nor shall any plague come near my dwelling."

The word **relief** means removal of something oppressive, painful, or distressing. Therefore, it is a good day for the new creation to remember and decree what Psalm 124:8 records.

Declaration:

Psalm 124:8—"Our help (relief) is in the name of the Lord, who made heaven and earth."

God reminds us in his word that he sends his angels before us to preserve a posterity for us in the earth, and to save our lives by a great deliverance. In our generation, we could say that some trust in their financial portfolio and some in their health status, but we trust in the name of the LORD our God to protect and deliver us from pandemics.

Trusting in our financial portfolio and health status is what we usually do when fear threatens to grab hold of our hearts. God is not surprised by the outbreak of plagues, pestilences, or troubles. He is not disinterested in our fears either. He is our rock, light, refuge, buckler, shield, salvation, and our great reward. Instead of looking to news stations and social media for support, this is the time to consider working the word of our Lord as commanded in Luke 21:28, "Now when you see these things begin to happen, look up and lift up your heads, because your redemption draws near".

In America, we are accustomed to power and security. Suddenly, as the possibility for reversal becomes greater, it is how we respond when we feel powerless and vulnerable that may offer the opportunity for us to mature and to witness this to others—something we say we long for. Jesus told us in Matthew 5:14-16 to "let our light shine in a dark world," and our response in a time such as this is to be such that kind of light and relief in a dark world.

CHAPTER 2

Fear

Fear is the antonym of faith. The Word of God says that faith comes by hearing and hearing the word of God. Likewise, fear comes by hearing and hearing information from the world. Circumstances by God's design are temporary and there may come a time when they are no longer effective. They all have an expiration date and will have to come to pass. To ensure a biblically rooted truth in circumstances that shall come to pass, note the phrase "and it came to pass" being seen many times in the scripture. This coronavirus pandemic shall pass, too.

I want you to know that before the coronavirus pandemic, there was an answer, healing, and a resolve for it. Soon, we will be able to say to coronavirus pandemic and every temporary circumstance that it, too, shall come to pass.

The world has dramatically changed. It is not business as usual anymore. As the world descends into turmoil, God commands the new creation to "fear not."

Declaration:

Psalm 23:4—"Yea, though I walk through the valley of the shadow of death, I will fear no evil; for You, Lord are with me."

Fear stifles and taints our lives of guilt. Fear torments. It hides, lurks, and lies in wait in concealment for an evil purpose. It controls until it is dealt with. What baffles me most is that we have yet a little knowledge of how fear has controlled humanity their whole lives. Today is a good day of deliverance from the evil of fear. Very little can be done under this spirit; it strangles and robs confidence to potential greatness. Fear is a dark shadow that envelops people and ultimately imprisons them within themselves. Many people have been prisoners of fear at one time or another, such as of uncertainty or death; but we can conquer fear by using the liberating word of the Lord that brings deliverance.

Fear's only cure is declaring, decreeing, and voice-activating God's word. Pouring ourselves out prayerfully is a life-changer! In Isaiah 41:10, the Holy Spirit inspired the prophet Isaiah to pen these wonderful words, "FEAR NOT, FOR I AM WITH YOU; BE NOT DISMAYED, FOR I AM YOUR GOD. I WILL STRENGTHEN YOU; YEA, I WILL HELP YOU, YEA, I WILL UPHOLD YOU WITH THE RIGHT HAND OF MY RIGHTEOUSNESS".

Declaration:

"I fear not, because You are with me. I am not dismayed because You are my God. You strengthen me. Yea, You help me. Yea, You uphold me with the right hand of Your righteousness."

2 Timothy 1:7 records that fear is not of God but rather comes by an evil spirit—that is, the spirit of fear—"For God has not given us the spirit of fear; but of power, and of love, and of a sound mind."

Declaration:

"Father, I declare I have the spirit of power, of love, and of a sound mind; and I walk in it every time."

We have to move out of our spiritual boxes and abandon the fear that constricts our souls.

Matthew 10:28 tells us who to fear and who not to fear—"And fear not them which kill the body, but are not able to kill the soul; but rather fear him which is able to destroy both soul and body in hell."

We read the encouraging words of Jesus in Luke 10:19, "Behold, I give unto you power to tread on serpents and scorpions, and over all the power of the enemy; and nothing shall by any means hurt you".

Declaration:

"Father, I acknowledge I have the power to tread on serpents and scorpions, and over all the power of the enemy. I declare nothing can by any means hurt me."

Prayer of faith causes all fear to be vanquished. Paul writes to the Philippians in Philippians 4:6–7 telling them, "⁶Be careful for nothing, but in everything by prayer and supplication with thanksgiving let your requests be made known unto God. ⁷And the peace of God, which passes all understanding, shall keep your hearts and minds through Christ Jesus".

Declaration:

"Devil, I declare to you on behalf of the new creation who you have caused to be fearful and unbelieving that we are not afraid of you. Devil, you can't manhandle the One to whom we are joined. I take authority over you and render you powerless, in the name of Jesus."

Are you facing fear today? Perhaps you are afraid of the coronavirus pandemic, of being debilitated by a health situation, or the uncertainty of the future. Don't allow fear to keep you from working the purpose of God in your life. God has kept you thus far; trust Him for the rest of the way. God wants His children **quiet from fear of evil.**

Meditating on God's word today is a life changer. Speaking the word of God back to him is a life changer. When you speak the word of God, the demons don't distinguish whether it is God speaking or you. All they hear is the word of God rebuking them. By voice-activating God's word, the angels harken to its voice and they do it with precision. God fulfills it. Yes, he performs it.

Proverbs 1:33—"But whoever listens to me will dwell safely, and will be secure, without fear of evil."

Declaration:

"Lord, I dwell safely because I listen to You and I am secure without fear of evil."

The fear of evil is vanquished as we draw nigh to God in faith—truly trusting him. We shall be quiet from the fear of evil, for no threatening of evil shall penetrate into the high tower of God. We are living in troubled and potentially very dangerous times, and divine guidance and intervention are of paramount importance. Threatening pestilences seem to be invading all areas of life from personal health, economic stability, to world peace that God has worked to establish. Troubled and dangerous times are nothing new in human history, but knowing how to handle the day of trouble or calamity is key to getting answers, resolves, and solutions for the child of God.

When a *crisis* comes, there is solace in the Scriptures. The only sure way of handling the day of trouble or calamity is by the word of God. The Lord is a consuming fire and he is destroying the adversary of his redeemed.

We read in the Bible in Jeremiah 23:29—"Is not My word like a fire?" says the LORD, "And like a hammer that breaks the rock in pieces?"

Declaration:

"I release the word of God in my atmosphere. I decree that God's word in my mouth is fire and a hammer and by it, I rebuke and eject fear out of my atmosphere."

This is the word of the Lord to the nations in Exodus 14:13—"Do not be afraid. Stand still, and see the salvation of the Lord, which He will accomplish for you today". For the coronavirus pandemic you see today, you shall see again no more forever.

COVID-19 is passing, too.

Declaration:

"Lord, I declare I am not afraid. I stand still and see the salvation which you accomplish for me today. The coronavirus pandemic I am seeing today—I shall see again no more forever. For you, Lord of hosts, said in Zechariah 4:6 that "it is not by might nor by power, but by Your Spirit just as You have said".

Declaration:

"Father, I acknowledge and declare your presence surrounding me in the hard places I am facing right now. May you, Lord, lead my way, and keep me secure, guide my steps forward, and cover me from behind. I receive the assurance that you are seeing me through as you work on my behalf, even behind the scenes where I can't fully see. Lord, I know beyond a doubt that you are faithful; that you turn my suffering around for good; and bring me forth as gold. I know your way and you call me by name."

COVID-19 is passing, too.

The Bible in Jeremiah 23:29 **declares that** "Is not My word like a fire?" says the Lord, "And like a hammer that breaks the rock in pieces?"

May God's presence surround you in the hard places you might be facing right now. May he lead your way and keep you secure, guide your steps forward, and cover you from behind. May he assure you that he is seeing you through as he works on your behalf, even behind the scenes where you can't fully see. Know beyond a doubt that our God is faithful; he will turn your suffering around for good somehow; and bring you forth as gold. He knows your way and he calls you by name.

CHAPTER 3

Faith vs Fear

> Luke 21:26—"....Men's hearts failing them from fear and the expectation of those things which are coming on the earth, for the powers of the heavens will be shaken."

That is not to say that men will have a heart attack or failure. People with carnal understanding may think that cardiovascular disease will increase. That is not what Jesus means, but he is figuratively saying that men's "hearts will be failing them from fear and the expectation of those things which are coming on the earth".

People are now fearful because of the COVID-19 pandemic. They are very much afraid. Fear comes just like faith comes.

Romans 10:17—"So then faith comes by hearing, and hearing by the word of God."

Similarly, fear comes by hearing and hearing the information from the world. Doubt is not the antonym of faith, but fear is. It implies that fear comes by hearing any words that do not come from God, which may be any words that are not in line with the revelation of the Word of God. That is how fear comes. Just like faith is not an emotion, fear also isn't. Faith is not out of the sensory nor fear.

2 Corinthians 5:7—"For we walk by faith, not by sight."

Just like faith is not in the sensory realm, fear is not in the sensory realm. Fear gives you a certain emotional state. People see our faith and attribute it as an emotion, thinking that we are arrogant. No! They are basically reading the emotional aspect of our faith—picking up on the emotional aspect of our spiritual force. Faith is in the spirit. For these people, what they see is confidence and therefore think that it is arrogance. They are attributing to our faith in the emotional state. Fear is the same way. If you have fear, it will manifest through your emotions. Just like faith is the condition of the heart, fear is also a condition of the heart.

Therefore, just like faith comes by hearing and by hearing the word of God, then fear also comes by speaking words that are not in line with the revelation of the Word of God. Men's hearts will be failing them for receiving information that is not from God. Listen to the news to get as much information as you need to know what is happening around the world, then turn it off. Do not let it keep coming to you. There isn't that much news, for literally, news doesn't go 24 hours. They keep speaking the same thing over and over again, filling you with fear, and the more you hear it, the more fear is affecting your spirit. The next thing you find yourself is starting to speak it.

This is one of the principles that govern the operations of the anointing. Faith goes out by what you speak, so if you don't want to be in fear, be silent right there and start declaring:

> Psalm 91:5–7—". . . .⁵I shall not be afraid of the terror by night, nor of the arrow that flies by day, ⁶ nor of the pestilence that walks in darkness, nor of the destruction that lays waste at noonday. ⁷A thousand may fall at my side, and ten thousand at my right hand, but it shall not come near me".
>
> Luke 21:26—"Expectation of those things which are coming on the earth."

You and I cannot afford to contribute to fear. We will have to guard our mouths. You and I must take a daily dose of Psalm 91 because those expectations coming daily from the earth bring fear.

Proverbs 24:10—"If you faint in the day of adversity, your strength is small."

If you are wavering now, it's not because you are an unbeliever; it's not because you don't trust God; but it's because the strength of your faith has diminished. As new creations in Christ Jesus, we have to guard our hearts with all diligence.

Proverbs 4:23—"Keep your heart with all diligence, for out of it spring the issues of life."

Forces of life are really the fruit of the Spirit.

Galatians 5:22-23—"But the fruit of the Spirit is love, joy, peace, longsuffering, kindness, goodness, faithfulness, [23] gentleness, self-control. Against such there is no law."

These are the forces of eternal life that are already within you. They are not coming in you, but they are in you. Now that it is in you, guard it because love and peace are flowing out from you. When Jesus met the woman at the well, he said it this way—the water that I give you will be in you a well of water springing up into everlasting life. So, you have to get what is springing up flowing out. You get it flowing out by what Jesus said in John 7:38, "He who believes in Me, as the Scripture has said, out of his heart will flow rivers of living water".

Now, I need scripture, but I don't particularly need it to have the well springing up nor need to know the word at all. All I need to know and do is to get saved. When I get saved, that's the time I get my well springing up. I need the well springing up to get rivers flowing out, so I can minister to other people. When I have the rivers flowing, I can keep my environment safe and immune. As a new creation, you are now the police of spiritual atmosphere of the universe. You have been deputized to police the atmosphere and are responsible to make sure you have a pandemic and fear-free zone as sons of God. The Bible reads in Romans 8:19-22:

"[19] For the earnest expectation of the creation eagerly waits for the revealing of the sons of God. [20] For the creation was subjected to futility, not willingly, but because of Him who subjected it in hope, [21] because the creation itself also will be delivered from the bondage of corruption into the glorious liberty of the children of God. [22] For we know that the whole creation groans and labors with birth pangs together until now."

The creation is waiting for what is going to come out of the sons. The whole creation is not waiting for the sons, but for the manifestation of what is to come out of them. It is waiting for what is in the sons to come out and change the atmosphere. We need to be strengthened with more faith when our strength is too small. The joy of the Lord which is in you strengthens you.

Nehemiah 8:10—". . . . Do not sorrow, for the joy of the Lord is your strength."

Therefore, we are to praise the Lord at our homes, not because we feel happy, but because we need a wellness dose in our faith. For that to happen, you need to turn off or shut off all the news from the media—Television, Facebook, Twitter, Instagram, Newsmongers, Gossipers, and Talebearers; and lift up your hands and start worshiping and rejoicing in the Lord; and take your wellness dose for strength.

We are living in the times where Jesus said that men's hearts will fail them because they are not strong enough spiritually to withstand the assault of the enemy coming against them.

Proverbs 18:4—"The words of a man's mouth are deep waters; The wellspring of wisdom is a flowing brook."

If a man's spirit is strong, it will sustain him or break him through. It will cause sickness to evaporate in the presence of the forces flowing out of his spirit. If the spirit of a man is strong enough, it will cause whatever is coming against him to disintegrate and will eat up the virus on its way out.

Romans 8:11—"But if the Spirit of Him who raised Jesus from the dead dwells in you, He who raised Christ from the dead will also give life to your mortal bodies through His Spirit who dwells in you."

The spirit of God dwells in him who is born again. That spirit will bring life to your mortal body. This is a higher level of news. The spirit of God is in your spirit and your spirit-man is in your body. When the Holy Spirit comes into the spirit of man, there is a well trying to spring out. The condition of your soul stops it from coming up. Your mind, will, emotion, and attitude stops it. If your mind is not renewed by God's word, your mind stops the well from springing forth. Your emotions stop it. Your will stops it. Your attitude stops it. All these decrease the fulness of the flow. This is because your mind is not renewed, which means you are not saying what God has said. You need to train your tongue to say what God has said. The more you get your mind renewed to God's word and speak in line with the word of God, the more that the well becomes a river springing out.

If now you employ the weapon of prayer in the spirit; that is, praying in tongues or in the spirit, then this will begin to flow in a greater propensity out of your mouth. Your healing from coronavirus is already within you. Your immunization from coronavirus is already within you. Your protection from the coronavirus is already within you. This is the good news of the principle that governs the operation of the anointing.

CHAPTER 4

Light in Darkness

In the wake of looming global crises, we are witnessing before our very eyes a day of trouble and distress; a day of devastation and desolation; a day of gloominess; and a day of clouds and thick darkness. We are in the genesis of a season of glooming plagues, pestilences, and trouble, all of which have come unexpectedly.

The children of God have light in their dwellings—the light and life of the gospel that **kindles in the darkness.** In seasons of dark moments of plagues, pestilences, and troubles, the sons of God are not without hope, but have a place of refuge to go for any present and future crises, including COVID-19. That place is described in the word of God, which reminds us where to put our trust for prevention and relief from plagues in case you are attacked. It is only God who can stop and heal a pandemic, but we must call on the Lord like a psalmist and declare.

Declaration:

Psalm 22:11—"Father be not far from me. For trouble is near. For there is none to help, but You."

The word **prevention** means obstruction, restraint, or discontinue. In the healthcare system, we say, "prevention is better than cure"; social distancing and quarantining explains it all.

The word **relief** means removal of something oppressive, painful, or distressing.

For the new creation, this is a good day to remember that "our help (relief) is in the name of the Lord, who made heaven and earth" as written in Psalm 124:8.

In Psalm 20:7, the psalmist reminds us that "Some trust in chariots and some in horses, but we trust in the name of the LORD our God". In our generation, we could say that some trust in their financial portfolio and some in their health status, but we trust in the name of the LORD our God.

Trusting in our financial portfolio and health status is what we usually do when fear threatens to grab hold of our hearts. God is not surprised by the outbreak of plagues, pestilences, or troubles. He is not disinterested in our fears either. He is our rock, light, refuge, buckler, shield, salvation, and our great reward. Instead of looking at news stations and social media for support, this is the time to consider the words of our Lord.

Luke 21:28—"Now when you see these things begin to happen, look up and lift up your heads, because your redemption draws near."

In America, we are accustomed to power and security. Suddenly, as the possibility for reversal becomes greater, it is how we respond when we feel powerless and vulnerable that may offer the opportunity for us to mature and to witness this to others—something we say we long for. Jesus told us in Matthew 5:14-16 to let our light shine in a dark world, and our response in a time such as this is to be such that kind of light and relief in a dark world.

CHAPTER 5

Signs of the Times and the End of the Age

Matthew 24:3–14—"³ Now as He sat on the Mount of Olives, the disciples came to Him privately, saying, "Tell us, when will these things be? And what will be the sign of Your coming, and of the end of the age?" ⁴ And Jesus answered and said to them: "Take heed that no one deceives you. ⁵ For many will come in My name, saying, 'I am the Christ,' and will deceive many. ⁶ And you will hear of wars and rumors of wars. See that you are not troubled; for all these things must come to pass, but the end is not yet. ⁷ For nation will rise against nation, and kingdom against kingdom. And there will be famines, pestilences, and earthquakes in various places. ⁸ All these are the beginning of sorrows. ⁹ "Then they will deliver you up to tribulation and kill you, and you will be hated by all nations for My name's sake. ¹⁰ And then many will be offended, will betray one another, and will hate one another. ¹¹ Then many false prophets will rise up and deceive many. ¹² And because lawlessness will abound, the love of many will grow cold. ¹³ But he who endures to the end shall be saved. ¹⁴ And this gospel of the kingdom will be preached in all the world as a witness to all the nations, and then the end will come."

Right now, the entire globe is in an uproar. People are genuinely praying. None of us thought we would ever see in our lifetime the great public perplexity, but here we are right in the center of it all. So, what is the word of God to us at this time? Government officials have said everything must shut down, and that businesses shut down unless they are a healthcare provider, news outlet, or emergency responder. Well, I am all three—a news outlet, a healthcare provider, and an emergency responder. I am transmitting the good news of Jesus Christ of Nazareth and ministering the healing grace of Jesus who heals all manner of sickness and disease among the people, including coronavirus. I am for miracles responding to emergency situations that only a miracle can accomplish. Uncertain times demand divine intervention in human affairs.

The church of Jesus Christ is a news outlet and a healthcare provider if you are standing on the word of God. If you are a child of the kingdom, now is not the time to be silent. You can prayerfully and financially support the work. There are three categories of calling that all the children of God fall into, relative to propagating the gospel of the kingdom. Some are called to literally go to the mission field. Others are called to send those who go by their giving (in tithes and offerings), and others are called to stay and pray. Some are called to two or three of these callings.

> Romans 10:14–15—"[14] How then shall they call on him in whom they have not believed? And how shall they believe in him of whom they have not heard? And how shall they hear without a preacher? [15] And how shall they preach, except they be sent? As it is written, 'How beautiful are the feet of them that preach the gospel of peace, and bring glad tidings of good things!'"

We are not going under but over the pandemic. The thing that is powerful to me as a son of the kingdom of God and as a man who studies the word of God is that I have God to be faithful. Jesus told us that these days would come and gave us instructions as to how you and I, as sons of the kingdom, should respond.

> Matthew 24:3—"Now as He sat on the Mount of Olives, the disciples came to Him privately, saying, 'Tell us, when will these things be? And what will be the sign of Your coming, and of the end of the age?'"

The world is not ending, but there is an age that is ending.

> Ezekiel 7:6–7—"⁶An end has come, the end has come; it has dawned for you; behold, it has come! ⁷Doom has come to you, you who dwell in the land."

The time has come, a day of trouble *is* near, and not of rejoicing in the mountains.

The world has shifted and changed. We are beholding an end of an age, modality, a way of living. Things have changed and will not go back to where they were. People are going different from the way they used to interact from right now and forward. Social distancing is going to remain long after COVID-19 is terminated. People are going to be looking at you to make sure you are clean.

Jesus said in Matthew 24:6 that "when you hear of wars and rumors of wars, see that you are not troubled; for all these things must come to pass, but the end is not yet." Your responsibility is to see to yourself that you are not troubled. Coronavirus is a pestilence, a cloud that is passing away, but the word of God is infinite.

Matthew 24:9 says—"Then they will deliver you up to tribulation and kill you, and you will be hated by all nations for My name's sake."

The word "tribulation" is a Greek word "Thlipsis" which means narrowness. Tribulation is not just some attack but being in a place of constraining or conflicting circumstances. There will be narrowness and limits to what you can do and where you can go. We are seeing it right now with lockdowns worldwide.

Jesus says the divine response and remedy to the things that are coming to the earth will be the gospel of the kingdom. It is not the gospel that Jesus saves. Of course, he does that, but this gospel of the kingdom is more than that Jesus saves.

CHAPTER 6

Signs in Heavens, Signals on Earth

Jesus himself told us the signs of the end of the age on earth would be distress of nations, with perplexity and men's hearts failing them from fear, and the expectation of those things which are coming on the earth. I believe this coronavirus pandemic is perplexity and is an indication of the end of an age.

> Luke 21:25-28—"^{25}There will be signs in the sun, in the moon, and in the stars; and on the earth distress of nations, with perplexity, the sea and the waves roaring; ^{26} men's hearts failing them from fear and the expectation of those things which are coming on the earth, for the powers of the heavens will be shaken. ^{27} Then they will see the Son of Man coming in a cloud with power and great glory. ^{28} Now when these things begin to happen, look up and lift up your heads, because your redemption draws near."

What happens in the heavens are a signal and an indication of what is going to happen on the earth. Daniel referred to the signs and wonders God does both in heaven and earth that "He (God) delivers and rescues, and He works signs and wonders. In heaven and on earth, who has delivered Daniel from the power of the lions" (Daniel 6:27).

Nations will be with distress and perplexity, which means the suffering will be so difficult to understand, causing confusion, and so complex that they will not have answers, solutions, nor resolves. Now is the time to hear from God's servants who are listening not just for analysis of problems, but for solutions of how God delivers and rescues.

> Exodus 14:1-2, 15-31—"¹Now the Lord spoke to Moses, saying: ² "Speak to the children of Israel,.... ¹⁵ And the Lord said to Moses, "Why do you cry to Me? Tell the children of Israel to go forward. ¹⁶ But lift up your rod, and stretch out your hand over the sea and divide it. And the children of Israel shall go on dry ground through the midst of the sea. ¹⁷ And I indeed will harden the hearts of the Egyptians, and they shall follow them. So I will gain honor over Pharaoh and over all his army, his chariots, and his horsemen. ¹⁸ Then the Egyptians shall know that I am the Lord, when I have gained honor for Myself over Pharaoh, his chariots, and his horsemen." ¹⁹ And the Angel of God, who went before the camp of Israel, moved and went behind them; and the pillar of cloud went from before them and stood behind them. ²⁰ So it came between the camp of the Egyptians and the camp of Israel. Thus it was a cloud and darkness to the one, and it gave light by night to the other, so that the one did not come near the other all that night. ²¹ Then Moses stretched out his hand over the sea; and the Lord caused the sea to go back by a strong east wind all that night, and made the sea into dry land, and the waters were divided. ²² So the children of Israel went into the midst of the sea on the dry ground, and the waters were a wall to them on their right hand and on their left. ²³ And the Egyptians pursued and went after them into the midst of the sea, all Pharaoh's horses, his chariots, and his horsemen. ²⁴ Now it came to pass, in the morning watch, that the Lord looked down upon the army of the Egyptians through the pillar of fire and cloud, and He troubled the

army of the Egyptians. ²⁵ And He took off their chariot wheels, so that they drove them with difficulty; and the Egyptians said, "Let us flee from the face of Israel, for the LORD fights for them against the Egyptians."

Moses' message remains relevant to us today. His calling is consistent with how God operates with every generation. God will not leave himself without a witness. The good news is that the Lord our God delivers and rescues us from pandemics by a mighty hand and by an outstretched arm.

> Acts 14:17—"Nevertheless, He did not leave Himself without witness, in that He did good, gave us rain from heaven and fruitful seasons, filling our hearts with food and gladness."

God chooses those he wishes to serve as his prophets. In spite of Moses' initial reluctance to serve as a prophet, he grew in his relationship with God and by the end of his life, he had successfully served in the role to which he was called.

Interestingly, Moses' relationship with God grew to the point that he received high praise from his Creator. When Miriam and Aaron spoke against Moses because of the Ethiopian woman whom he had married, God revealed his assessment of Moses.

> Numbers 12:1—"Then Moses stretched out his hand over the sea; and the LORD caused the sea to go back by a strong east wind all that night, and made the sea into dry land, and the waters were divided."

Speaking directly to Moses' brother Aaron and sister Miriam, God said:

> Numbers 12:6-8—"Hear now My words: If there is a prophet among you, I, the LORD, make Myself known

to him in a vision; I speak to him in a dream. Not so with My servant Moses, he is faithful in all My house. I speak with him face to face, even plainly, and not in dark sayings; and he sees the form of the LORD. Why then were you not afraid to speak against My servant Moses?"

Acts 3:22-26—"²²For Moses truly said to the fathers, 'The Lord your God will raise up for you a Prophet like me from your brethren. Him you shall hear in all things, whatever He says to you. 23 And it shall be that every soul who will not hear that Prophet shall be utterly destroyed from among the people.' 24 Yes, and all the prophets, from Samuel and those who follow, as many as have spoken, have also foretold[b] these days. 25 You are sons of the prophets, and of the covenant which God made with our fathers, saying to Abraham, 'And in your seed all the families of the earth shall be blessed.'"

I declare the plague will be stayed and not spread any further. It will pass over us. I declare with Isaiah 8:18—"wherever the Lord sends us on a mission, the plague will pass over us. Here am I and the children whom the LORD has given me! We are for signs and wonders in the earth".

Jeremiah 32:20–22—"²⁰You have set signs and wonders in the land of Egypt, to this day, and in Israel and among other men; and You have made Yourself a name, as it is this day. ²¹ You have brought Your people Israel out of the land of Egypt with signs and wonders, with a strong hand and an outstretched arm, and with great terror; ²² You have given them this land, of which You swore to their fathers to give them—"a land flowing with milk and honey."

Deuteronomy 14:13–14, 26–31—"¹³And Moses said to the people, "Do not be afraid. Stand still, and see the salvation of the LORD, which He will accomplish for you today. For the Egyptians whom you see today, you shall see again no more forever. [14] The LORD will fight for you, and you shall hold your peace." [26] Then the LORD said to Moses, "Stretch out your hand over the sea, that the waters may come back upon the Egyptians, on their chariots, and on their horsemen." [27] And Moses stretched out his hand over the sea; and when the morning appeared, the sea returned to its full depth, while the Egyptians were fleeing into it. So the LORD overthrew[f] the Egyptians in the midst of the sea. [28] Then the waters returned and covered the chariots, the horsemen, and all the army of Pharaoh that came into the sea after them. Not so much as one of them remained. [29] But the children of Israel had walked on dry land in the midst of the sea, and the waters were a wall to them on their right hand and on their left. [30] So the LORD saved[g] Israel that day out of the hand of the Egyptians, and Israel saw the Egyptians dead on the seashore. [31] Thus Israel saw the great work which the LORD had done in Egypt; so the people feared the LORD, and believed the LORD and His servant Moses."

We need people who will speak responsibly and discern where the information is coming from.

CHAPTER 7

Jesus, the Solid Rock

Matthew 7:24–27—"²⁴Therefore whoever hears these sayings of Mine, and does them, I will liken him to a wise man who built his house on the rock: ²⁵ and the rain descended, the floods came, and the winds blew and beat on that house; and it did not fall, for it was founded on the rock. ²⁶ "But everyone who hears these sayings of Mine, and does not do them, will be like a foolish man who built his house on the sand: ²⁷ and the rain descended, the floods came, and the winds blew and beat on that house; and it fell. And great was its fall."

Jesus, the Solid Rock, is the only foundation that will stand when the storms arise; the only foundation to build our lives on.

1 Peter 1:23 says, "For you have been born again, not of perishable seed, but of imperishable, through the living and enduring word of God." That is the foundation. When a man hears the Gospel, believes the Gospel, and becomes a doer of the Gospel, Christ, the Solid Rock, becomes the foundation of that life.

Men's words cannot endure forever. Whosoever, therefore, builds his life on the word and ideology of men will collapse. The principle of the world is like sand easily drifted by the time. Men change and so do their words, ideology, and policies. It is only wise that we build our life on the word of God because it does not change, and it does not fail.

Building on Christ the solid rock means to live by the Word of God which is Christ. Only those who believe the Word of God will be building on a solid foundation. After the foundation has been laid, we must continue to build with the Word of God. The Word of God is both the bricks and the cement that holds everything together. We must build every aspect of our life on it. Christ is the true foundation.

Religion will fail, philosophy will falter, atheism will fall, knowledge will be flawed, and man's wisdom will become foolish with time, but only Christ, the solid foundation, will remain!

Building our lives on the Word of God, which is Christ, is the only wise thing to do. Resist the temptation to build your life on anything else; it will not stand the trouble and the test of time. It will lead to regret, sorrow, and loss. You are the temple of the Lord and such a sacred structure must be built according to the pattern given by God himself. That was exactly what Moses did in the wilderness.

Hebrews 8:5 says, "Moses was warned when he was about to build the tabernacle: "See to it that you make everything according to the pattern shown you on the mountain".

As Moses was faithful in building the tabernacle, we must be faithful in building our life, the temple of God according to the word of God. Whatever you are building in life—a family, a career, a business, a house, children or an idea, let it be known to you that Christ is the surest foundation, and all other ground is sinking sand!

Humans have limitations. With man, many things are not possible, but with God, nothing shall be impossible! Do you know Christ? Do you have Christ? Do you know that he is the solid and surest foundation you can build on? Have you attempted to build on him? Would you say with the psalmist in Psalm 119:114, "You are my hiding place and my shield, I hope in Your word"?

You may be dealing with some situations, plagues, pestilences, or some sorts of troubles, and feel like all the hope is gone. I present Jesus, the Solid Rock, to you to build on. He will give you hope of glory and you will then be able to survive the storms of life! You will truly sing:

1. My hope is built on nothing less
   Than Jesus' blood and righteousness;
   I dare not trust the sweetest frame,
   But wholly lean on Jesus' name.

   Refrain:

   On Christ, the solid Rock, I stand;
   All other ground is sinking sand,
   All other ground is sinking sand.

2. When darkness veils His lovely face,
   I rest on His unchanging grace;
   In every high and stormy gale,
   My anchor holds within the veil.

3. His oath, His covenant, His blood
   Support me in the whelming flood;
   When all around my soul gives way,
   He then is all my hope and stay.

4. When He shall come with trumpet sound,
   Oh, may I then in Him be found;
   Dressed in His righteousness alone,
   Faultless to stand before the throne.

Isaiah 28:16—"Therefore thus says the Lord God: 'Behold, I lay in Zion a stone for a foundation, a tried stone, a precious cornerstone, a sure foundation; Whoever believes will not act hastily.'"

CHAPTER 8

Eliminate the Enemy

God has given the new creation authority to his children to defeat and destroy pandemics. The ministry of Jesus in earth was teaching, preaching, and healing. He commissioned his followers to continue the work in the same manner of articulation.

> Luke 10:19—"Behold, I give you the authority to trample on serpents and scorpions, and over all the power of the enemy, and nothing shall by any means hurt you."

In the Bible in 2 Chronicles 7:14, God tells us the manner in which we are to deal with pandemics, and that is, by prayer of faith—"If My people who are called by My name will humble themselves, and pray and seek My face, and turn from their wicked ways, then I will hear from heaven, and will forgive their sin and heal their land".

Notice that God wants us to approach him with attitude of humility and prayer; seeking his face and turning from wicked ways. His response will be hearing, forgiving sins, and healing the land.

The prayer of faith is voice-activating or sending God's word to the pandemic.

> Matthew 8:5–8, 13—"Now when Jesus had entered Capernaum, a centurion came to Him, pleading with Him, ⁶ saying, "Lord, my servant is lying at home

paralyzed, dreadfully tormented." ⁷ And Jesus said to him, "I will come and heal him." ⁸ The centurion answered and said, "Lord, I am not worthy that You should come under my roof. But only speak a word, and my servant will be healed. ¹³ Then Jesus said to the centurion, "Go your way; and as you have believed, so let it be done for you." And his servant was healed that same hour."

It is time for some healing of our land. The healing of our land won't manifest through fear, but faith.

Prayer is an act of humility because it declares that you and I in ourselves are not in control of these formidable issues and we need the help of God.

Exercising social distancing and quarantining is not a hindrance to sending people the prevention and relief they desperately need in a time of a pandemic. It creates an opportunity to send healing prayer to whoever is suffering from whatever disease they are suffering—the land, businesses, marriages, and families.

It is time to **_eliminate the enemies' pandemic plans_**! God is opening up the windows of heaven to give you clear spiritual insight concerning your next move, pertaining to your destiny in the wake of pestilences. God is positioning you to get in front of the enemy and destroy everything including COVID-19 that the enemy tries to put in your way to destiny by prayer of faith.

When the world is panicking and fearful, it is an appropriate time to **_eliminate the enemy_**! You may be asking yourself, "What does **_'eliminate the enemy'_** mean?" When you **_eliminate the enemy,_** you are exposing the enemy's tactics and moving them out of the way through the declaration of God's written and Rhema Word.

I know that prophetic words have been spoken over your life, but this time, you will step out in faith with revelation knowledge and declare what God has destined for your life. This time, you will activate the power of the Anointed One and **_eliminate the enemy._**

Every time you voice-activate the word of God, you are praying and receiving clear vision in how to out the enemy. No more delay! Today, stand firm on the Word of God and *eliminate the enemy.*

You may have asked God, "How long is the COVID-19 pandemic going to last?" You need to *eliminate the enemy* and declare that no plague shall come near your dwelling. You may have wondered, *"When will I see blessing coming to my home?"* You need to *eliminate the enemy* and declare that the blessing rests on you and your household!

You may have been asking the question, "Why has the dry season persisted this long?" You need to *eliminate the enemy* and declare that God is giving you increase more and more!

You might have been told it will never happen, but I'm here to tell you it's already done as you *eliminate the enemy* and stand in the authority you've been given through the finished work of Jesus. Whatever you do today, know this—every time you declare the Word of God, you are eliminating the enemy. You are dismantling the enemies' plans with every Word of God that you speak.

CHAPTER 9

Wisdom that Governs Anointing Operations

> James 3:14–17—"¹⁴ But if you have bitter envy and self-seeking in your hearts, do not boast and lie against the truth. ¹⁵ This wisdom does not descend from above, but is earthly, sensual, demonic. ¹⁶ For where envy and self-seeking exist, confusion and every evil thing are there. ¹⁷ But the wisdom that is from above is first pure, then peaceable, gentle, willing to yield, full of mercy and good fruits, without partiality and without hypocrisy."

This time of the pandemic outbreak, the children of the kingdom are to be manifesting heavenly characters. The gospel of the kingdom is supposed to be preached as evidence. Evidence is going to be manifesting for people who are actually trusting in God's word as opposed to people who are simply going to church. Evidence will be manifesting that will distinguish people who are standing on the word and people who are just attending church. If you are standing on the word of God, you are not afraid of coronavirus. There are church attenders that are shaking, being afraid of it. It is important to understand that the government leaders are operating according to the carnal information they have. We as the children of the kingdom have access to the information they cannot access.

James is articulating universal principles that are supposed to be understood by the new creation as relates to the operations of the spirit world and its dimension. The wisdom that comes from the earth is the wisdom that comes from the senses. It is the product of human intellect, education, analysis, and observation. People are saying what they see, surmise, and deduce with intellectual educational reasoning, but that is only the reasoning that comes from the earth. It is sensual or from the senses. They tell you what they feel, think, fear, or what terror they have within them. Some of the stuff they are saying is actually coming from demons. They are doctrines of demons. This is the education of demons to get you and keep you in fear.

Here is what the word of God is saying—the only thing the world has is the wisdom from three sources. It is either from their intellect, senses, or from demons and they are just repeating it. Just like you and I repeat what comes to us from the spirit of God our Father, they are repeating what comes to them from the spirit of their father, the devil. I don't know about you, but I am not going to live my life according to intellectual wisdom, sensory wisdom, or demon wisdom.

As you and I are children of the kingdom, we say "no, we will not bow to them," declaring what God has recorded in Psalm 91:7, "A thousand may fall at your side, and ten thousand at your right hand; but it shall not come near you".

We are rejecting demon wisdom, intellectual wisdom, and sensory wisdom. Let us read James 3:15 and please notice what God says, "This wisdom does not descend from above, but is earthly, sensual, demonic".

James 3:17—"But the wisdom that is from above is first pure, then peaceable, gentle, willing to yield, full of mercy and good fruits, without partiality and without hypocrisy."

Please understand that God is telling us as new creations that there is wisdom that comes from beneath and that there is also wisdom that comes from above. You have the right as a new creation to live either by the wisdom that comes from beneath or by the wisdom that comes from above. Now, the world only has the option of living by the wisdom that comes from beneath. They don't yet have access to the level of the wisdom that comes from above. That is why in times of perplexity, they are saying things differently from what we are saying., which is why we will also continue saying things differently from what they are saying. There is a line drawn here!

Isaiah 53:1—"Who has believed our report? And to whom has the arm of the LORD been revealed?"

Will you believe the report that comes from beneath or that comes from above, and live by that wisdom? When the world is operating on the wisdom that is earthly, the child of God operates on the wisdom whose source is God.

Let us read James 3:17 in Amplified version:

> James 3:17—"But the wisdom from above is first pure [morally and spiritually undefiled], then peace-loving [courteous, considerate], gentle, reasonable [and willing to listen], full of compassion and good fruits. It is unwavering, without [self-righteous] hypocrisy [and self-serving guile]."

The wisdom that is from above is the word of God. It comes from God. It is consistent and unchangeable no matter when you tap into it. It is the same. It is true when he says he was wounded for our transgressions. It is true when there is coronavirus and when it is not there. The presence of coronavirus does not change the wisdom of God. It is pure—plagues, pestilences, and pandemics cannot contaminate the wisdom from above. The wisdom of God overcomes catastrophe, calamity, plagues, pandemics, pestilences, disease, virus, bacteria, malady, and malfunction. It is pure. This wisdom that comes from above is the information that is to govern the operation of the anointing for the new creation.

> 1 Corinthians 1:18–25 (amp)—"¹⁸ For the message of the cross is foolishness [absurd and illogical] to those who are perishing and spiritually dead [because they reject it], but to us who are being saved [by God's grace] it is [the manifestation of] the power of God. ¹⁹ For it is written and forever remains written,
>
> "I will destroy the wisdom of the wise [the philosophy of the philosophers],
>
> And the cleverness of the clever [who do not know Me] I will nullify."
>
> ²⁰ Where is the wise man (philosopher)? Where is the scribe (scholar)? Where is the debater (logician, orator) of this age? Has God not exposed the foolishness of this world's wisdom? ²¹ For since the world through all its [earthly] wisdom failed to recognize God, God in His wisdom was well-pleased through the [a]foolishness of the message preached [regarding salvation] to save those who believe [in Christ and welcome Him as Savior]. ²² For Jews demand signs (attesting miracles), and Greeks pursue [worldly] wisdom and philosophy, ²³ but we preach Christ crucified, [a message which is] to Jews a stumbling block [that provokes their opposition], and to Gentiles foolishness [just utter nonsense], ²⁴ but to those who are the called, both Jews and Greeks (Gentiles), Christ is the power of God and the wisdom of God. ²⁵ [This is] because the foolishness of God [is not foolishness at all and] is wiser than men [far beyond human comprehension], and the weakness of God is stronger than men [far beyond the limits of human effort]."

The message of what the cross of Jesus has done is a benefit to those who are being saved. The message of the cross for those of us who have been born again gives us access to the power of God. The more I know of what the cross of Jesus accomplished, the more access I have to the power of God.

I Corinthians 1:19—"For it is written and forever remains written, 'I WILL DESTROY THE WISDOM OF THE WISE [the philosophy of the philosophers], AND THE CLEVERNESS OF THE CLEVER [who do not know Me] I WILL NULLIFY.'"

Right now, the wisdom of the wise is being destroyed. It is clear evidence that all the stuff that you and I trusted in systematically cannot sustain and support us. We got the wisest minds—the most intelligent, articulate minds the world can offer—but what they are telling us is 'we are doing the best we can'. They are telling us, "Wash your hands". Well, that is prudent.

We preach what was accomplished by crucifixion, resurrection, accession, and sitting of Jesus Christ to the Jews and Greeks, but to them, it is foolishness. However, to those who are called both Jews and Greeks (Gentiles), Christ is both the power and wisdom of God. So, knowing that God has accomplished through Jesus Christ at the cross, then I already am receiving the wisdom of God. Now it is my choice whether I am going to live by God's wisdom or the other wisdom. Now us new creations are being asked by God to choose which wisdom we will live by. This is what this time is. Hear what the spirit is saying 'what wisdom you are going to live by from this time forward'. Some of us have made the decision already.

The foolishness of God is wiser than men's wisdom of washing hands and social distancing. When men call what you and I do for God as foolishness, he calls it wiser than men's wisdom. If I tell you to do what God has said, it is wiser than what men have told you. I am not telling you to disregard wise counsels—please comply as much as lies within you. However, I am not trusting their guidelines because there are people with masks and personal protective equipment contracting coronavirus, too.

Proverbs 21:30 —"There is no [human] wisdom or understanding or counsel [that can prevail] against the LORD."

If somebody tells you this is wisdom, but that wisdom goes against God's word, then that is not wisdom. If somebody tells you this is understanding, but that wisdom goes against God's word, then that as well is not wisdom. They don't understand. If somebody gives you counsel that goes against God's word, God tells you that you have not been properly counseled. That is why the Holy Spirit is telling us there is no human wisdom, understanding, or counsel that can prevail against the Lord. I am not telling you that wearing a mask is a bad idea, but when the government or the medical practitioner tells you that communion (partaking of the Lord's table) won't help you, then I call them a fool and a liar. I am not calling just anybody a fool and a liar, and don't you call me one when I tell God's people what his word says. You can tell your people don't assemble; that is your wisdom. I tell my people forsake not the assembling of yourselves together.

> Hebrews 10:25—"25 not forsaking our meeting together [as believers for worship and instruction], as is the habit of some, but encouraging one another; and all the more [faithfully] as you see the day [of Christ's return] approaching."

I am not defying you, but I am simply going by my wisdom. Now I will comply with you as long as the spirit of God allows me. But if you tell me not to gather and the spirit of God tells me to gather, you better call the police. I will today and throughout and after this pandemic, work in the wisdom of God.

> 1 Corinthians 2:4-101 (AMP)—"4 And my message and my preaching were not in persuasive words of wisdom [using clever rhetoric], but [they were delivered] in demonstration of the [Holy] Spirit [operating through me] and of [His] power [stirring the minds of the listeners and persuading them], 5 so that your faith would not rest on the wisdom and rhetoric of men, but on the power of

God. ⁶ Yet we do speak wisdom among those spiritually mature [believers who have teachable hearts and a greater understanding]; but [it is a higher] wisdom not [the wisdom] of this present age nor of the rulers and leaders of this age, who are passing away; ⁷ but we speak God's wisdom in a mystery, the wisdom once hidden [from man, but now revealed to us by God, that wisdom] which God predestined before the ages to our glory [to lift us into the glory of His presence]. ⁸ None of the rulers of this age recognized and understood this wisdom; for if they had, they would not have crucified the Lord of glory; ⁹ but just as it is written [in Scripture], "THINGS WHICH THE EYE HAS NOT SEEN AND THE EAR HAS NOT HEARD, AND WHICH HAVE NOT ENTERED THE HEART OF MAN, ALL THAT GOD HAS PREPARED FOR THOSE WHO LOVE HIM [who hold Him in affectionate reverence, who obey Him, and who gratefully recognize the benefits that He has bestowed]." ¹⁰ For God has unveiled them and revealed them to us through the [Holy] Spirit; for the Spirit searches all things [diligently], even [sounding and measuring] the [profound] depths of God [the divine counsels and things far beyond human understanding]."

Now we are getting to it. One of the reasons of what is happening in the church is because we have immature Christians who cannot actually receive the wisdom of God. When you give them the wisdom and the counsel of God, they won't receive it. The wisdom and the rule of this age is coming to nothing. God has been holding this wisdom for us from before the foundations of the earth. He has been holding this wisdom to be released in these hours so that the wheat and tares can be separated; so that the real children of God and of the wicked one can be discerned. This is the hidden wisdom which God ordained before the world.

CHAPTER 10

Prophet Priest and King

> 1 Timothy 2:1–4—"Therefore I exhort first of all that supplications, prayers, intercessions, and giving of thanks be made for all men, ² for kings and all who are in authority, that we may lead a quiet and peaceable life in all godliness and reverence. ³ For this is good and acceptable in the sight of God our Savior, ⁴ who desires all men to be saved and to come to the knowledge of the truth."

God in heaven rules over all the kingdoms of nations by three anointings—the Prophet, the Priest, and the King—to accomplish his agenda in all the earth. He changes the times and the seasons. He removes kings and raises up others. He gives wisdom to the wise and knowledge to those who have understanding.

> 2 Chronicles 20:6—"The Lord God is God in heaven, and rules over all the kingdoms of the nations, and in His hand there is power and might, so that no one is able to withstand Him."
>
> Psalm 22:28—"For the kingdom is the Lord's, and He rules over the nations."

We don't just pray, intercede, and supplicate, but also give thanks for the answers. The kings include our present-day presidents, prime ministers, governors, mayors, legislatures, and judicial officials. Those in authority are the five multifaceted ministry giftings—apostles, prophets, evangelists, pastors, and teachers. We are commanded by the Holy Spirit to supplicate, pray, intercede, and give thanks for both secular and spiritual leaders. It doesn't matter whether we like them or not. It doesn't matter whether we agree with them or not. God says we need to pray for them. We have to do this because they have authority to make decisions that can alter your life and mine. God wants you and I as his people to live a quiet and peaceable life. We pray so the government officials and those in authority do not begin to pass laws and regulations that interrupt the quiet and peaceable life of people, including the redeemed, which is the reason that God tells you and I to pray for kings and those in authority. Most of the church do not pray for their leaders because they don't agree with their policies. What you need to understand is that right now, they are in power and have the authority to make decisions that will affect your life and mine.

God governs the universe and earth by the wisdom of his word. He has shared it among three offices that govern his affairs—the Prophet, Priest and King. These three work hand in hand.

> Proverbs 3:19-20—"The LORD by wisdom founded the earth; by understanding He established the heavens; [20] by His knowledge the depths were broken up, and clouds drop down the dew."

We pray for leaders so they may be hearing the counsel, wisdom, and spirit of God.

God's objective for us praying for the leaders is that everybody gets saved. God wants everybody to be born again. God doesn't want people in leadership to make decisions that hinder the liberty of the gospel.

We must remember that the federal, state, and local government cannot prohibit worship because the constitution states that it separates the state from the church. However, there is no complete separation of church and the state. The people of God have the responsibility to speak into government. God's order of governance was made up of three anointings—the King, the Prophet, and the Priest.

> 1 Kings 1:45—"So Zadok the priest and Nathan the prophet have anointed him king at Gihon; and they have gone up from there rejoicing, so that the city is in an uproar. This is the noise that you have heard."

The prophet had the responsibility of understanding the times, to know what Israel ought to do. The priest had the responsibility of anointing the king to install him to office, and the king's responsibility was to enforce what God had said. It is important that the people of God stay connected through the divine medium of communication these days.

What is in danger of happening right now all over the globe is that if God's people don't pray, people in leadership who are listening to the counsel of the adversary, doctrines of demons, and natural information will begin to make decisions that hinder the liberty of preaching the gospel, and therefore, people will be hindered from coming to salvation; but we as the body of Christ are going to say "hell No!" or in this context, we mean "no to hell"—you are not going to advance and hinder the gospel.

We are in the last days and people need to hear the gospel. Many people don't agree with their leaders, but one thing is clear—there is a move that is preparing for the antichrist, the man of sin to be revealed. Pervasive mindset is for a one-world government, a one-world religion, and a one-world economy. What we have been calling populism and nationalism actually are leaders who have been resisting that spirit, not going along with everything that has been going on everywhere in the world. We do not understand this, but let me tell you—when you are somewhere you are unable to preach, then you will wish that you had prayed. When you are in a situation where you are unable to go outside the house until some military individuals tell you that you now can, then you will wish that you had prayed. This is happening in a lot of nations of the world. One thing that has disturbed me most is that when you look at nations and the alignment of nations that have been spoken about at the end times, United States of America does not show up anywhere. That may possibly mean that if people of God don't pray, United Nations shall be absorbed in some sort of global entity and we lose our sovereignty and ability to make decisions. It is time for the church to pray. I am not afraid, though, of what is going on because if it gets too bad, my household, I, and the spiritual children God has given me will be out of here. Yeah, Jesus is coming back and we shall be on the record. You will be reading this book when we are gone, but right now, we must pray that another whole set of godly spiritual counsel will get access to our leaders; for the church also got secular, religious puppets, speaking into the counsel of governmental leaders. We have a lot of people with political ideologies rather than spiritual insights who are counseling our governmental leaders. Governmental leaders need people around them who shall speak to them the word of God. I know that there are already a couple of them, but God knows that leaders need some more.

Jesus said in Matthew 4:4—"It is written, 'Man shall not live by bread alone, but by every word that proceeds from the mouth of God.'"

There is a word proceeding or coming forth from the mouth of God through his men and women who are connected to him and we all need to hear it, especially in these times of public perplexity of COVID-19. The church of Jesus Christ will be strong to pray, intercede, supplicate, and give thanks for the victory so the leaders can hear, declare, and make informed decisions.

The Anointing Establishes Dominion

This gospel is the good news that governs the operation of the anointing. The anointing of God is how God establishes dominion. God establishes his kingdom on earth by the anointing. In the old testament, it was the prophet, king, and the priest who were anointed. If the anointing was not on you, you couldn't hold an office to oversee or speak from. Until now, God requires anointing. The anointing of God has to do with understanding the principles that govern his operations. The anointing was the good news giving you the authority to operate God's affairs. We have the authority to operate the anointing, and I don't have to wait for God to show up. As a son of God, I have his nature, character, and authority in the earth to operate the anointing; to give it direction; and to tell it where to go and what to do there. The gospel tells you "don't wait for God to do it", so it has to be preached. You have the authority to do it. Christ in you is the hope of glory as recorded in Colossians 1:27—"To them God has chosen to make known among the Gentiles the glorious riches of this mystery, which is Christ in you, the hope of glory".

Prayer for the Government

1 Timothy 2:1–3—Father, in the name of Jesus, we thank you for the United States and its government. We hold up in prayer before you those in positions of leadership. We pray and intercede for the president, the representatives, the senators, the judges of our land, governors and mayors, and all those in leadership over us in any way, as well as the armed forces and the police force. We pray that the spirit of the Lord rests upon them.

Proverbs 2:10–12, 21–22—We declare skillful and godly wisdom enters into the heart of our president and that knowledge be pleasant to him; discretion watches over him; knowledge keeps him and delivers him from the way of evil and from evil men. Father, we ask you to compass the president with men and women who make their hearts and ears attentive to godly counsel and do that which is right in your sight. We believe that you cause them to be men and women of integrity who are obedient concerning us, that we may lead a quiet and peaceable life in all godliness and honesty. We pray that the upright shall dwell in our government. May men and women, blameless and complete in your sight, shall remain in these positions of authority, but the wicked shall be cut off from our government and the treacherous are rooted out of it.

Psalm 33:12—Father, your word declares that "blessed is the nation whose God is their Lord". We receive your blessing.

Psalms 9:9—Father, you are our refuge and stronghold in times of trouble, high cost, destitution, and desperation.

Deuteronomy 28:10–11—So we declare with our mouth that your people dwell safely in this land, and we prosper abundantly.

Romans 8:37—We are more than conquerors through Christ Jesus and nothing can separate us from your love.

Proverbs 21:1—Father, you have said in your word that the heart of the king is in the hand of the Lord and you turn it whichever way you desire. We believe the hearts of our leaders are in your hand and that their decisions are divinely directed by you.

Acts 12:24—Thank you Lord because the good news of the gospel is published in our land. Thank you Lord because your word prevails and grows mightily in the hearts and lives of the people. Thank you for this land and the leaders you have given to us. Jesus, you are Lord over United States of America!

In the name of Jesus of Nazareth, we count it done, and it is so. Amen.

CHAPTER 11

Church is at Your House

The church met at the house to worship. In other words, the church met in their various houses to hear God's word, make supplications, prayers of faith, intercessions, *and* giving of thanks for all men, kings, and all in authority, that they would lead a quiet and peaceable life in all godliness and reverence which was good and acceptable in the sight of God our Savior. They continued daily with one accord in the temple, and breaking bread from house to house, they ate their food with gladness and simplicity of heart, praising God and having favor with all the people, and the Lord added to the church daily those who were being saved. The true spiritual husband was the priest at the house to lead his wife and family into a daily worship experience. Spiritual wives, mothers, and grandmothers like Eunice and Lois (2 Timothy 1:5) and Mary (Acts 12:12) would fill in lest the household be cut off from divine connection. Having church in the house was convenient, and worship was without haste. They would pray overnight and as long as it required to get a miracle going. We see this in the Bible in Acts 12:1-18 at the house of Mary where many were gathered together praying. Verse 5 says "Peter was therefore kept in prison, but constant prayer was offered to God for him by the church".

The situations we are in now is demanding preachers of the gospel to do more than sermonize to Christians. You have to be coming with the word of God that will stabilize people, give them hope, and strength; and demand they are not dependent on you. This is true because now, you have to operate from your house. Now, you have to get together with your family because you cannot get out. If you don't know how to partake of the Lord's table (communion) in your own house, you are in trouble. If you don't know how to worship God in your own house, you are in trouble. God is demanding by his Spirit that the church get back to the original pattern. The original pattern of the church was not global gatherings in arenas, it was from house to house. They had church at the house. I will qualify that by the following references in the Bible.

Acts 8:3—"³ As for Saul, he made havoc of the church, entering every house, and dragging off men and women, committing them to prison."

Saul knew where to find the believers who were worshipping in truth and Spirit—in the houses. Originally, the church was meeting in houses to worship. Therefore, he was having easy time finding them and accomplishing the religious agenda of making havoc of the church by entering every house and dragging off men and women, committing them to prison.

> Romans 16:5 —"Likewise greet **the church that is in their house**...."
>
> 1 Corinthians 16:19—"The churches of Asia greet you. Aquila and Priscilla greet you heartily in the Lord, with the church that is in their house."
>
> Colossians 4:15 —"Greet the brethren who are in Laodicea, and Nymphas and the church that is in his house."
>
> Philemon 1:2 —"To **the beloved** Apphia, Archippus our fellow soldier, and to the church in your house."
>
> Acts 2:46 —"So continuing daily with one accord in the temple, and breaking bread from house to house, they ate their food with gladness and simplicity of heart."

> Acts 20:18–21—"¹⁸ And when they had come to him, he said to them: "You know, from the first day that I came to Asia, in what manner I always lived among you, ¹⁹ serving the Lord with all humility, with many tears and trials which happened to me by the plotting of the Jews; ²⁰ how I kept back nothing that was helpful, but proclaimed it to you, and taught you publicly and from house to house, ²¹ testifying to Jews, and also to Greeks, repentance toward God and faith toward our Lord Jesus Christ."

Therefore, it is comprehensible and unmistakable that the church has never been about buildings. When they came together for public worship, the power of God fell because they knew how to worship in their houses and had church already in the house.

Believe it or not, the many orders and restrictive measures that have been released through our national, federal, state, and local governments relative to the gathering of people around the earth is God's way of demanding by his Spirit that the church get back to the original pattern he established so that the foundations are not destroyed.

> 2 Timothy 2:19—"Nevertheless the solid foundation of God stand sure, having this seal: "The Lord knows those who are His, and, Let everyone who names the name of [Christ depart from iniquity."

CHAPTER 12

Communion at the House

1 Corinthians 10:14–22—"¹⁴ Therefore, my beloved, flee from idolatry. ¹⁵ I speak as to wise men; judge for yourselves what I say. ¹⁶ The cup of blessing which we bless, is it not the [e]communion of the blood of Christ? The bread which we break, is it not the communion of the body of Christ? ¹⁷ For we, though many, are one bread and one body; for we all partake of that one bread. ¹⁸ Observe Israel after the flesh: Are not those who eat of the sacrifices [f]partakers of the altar? ¹⁹ What am I saying then? That an idol is anything, or what is offered to idols is anything? ²⁰ Rather, that the things which the Gentiles sacrifice they sacrifice to demons and not to God, and I do not want you to have fellowship with demons. ²¹ You cannot drink the cup of the Lord and the cup of demons; you cannot partake of the Lord's table and of the table of demons. ²² Or do we provoke the Lord to jealousy? Are we stronger than He? ²³ All things are lawful [that is, morally legitimate, permissible], but not all things are beneficial or advantageous. All things are lawful, but not all things are constructive [to character] and edifying [to spiritual life]. ²⁴ Let no one seek [only] his own good, but [also] that of the other person. ²⁵ [Regarding meat offered to idols:] Eat anything that is sold in the meat market without asking any questions for the sake of your conscience…"

Get away from image, idea, or any forms of idolatry that you are trusting in which God has not erected. Any idea or opinion that you are trusting in that doesn't come from God—don't trust them in times of trouble. God is speaking to people who have access to the wisdom of God to stop bowing down to these images of worldly wisdom. All of us who are new creations of Jesus Christ are living from the finished work of resurrected Christ.

1 John 4:17—". . . . As He is, so are we in this present world."

We are living from the finished work of Christ. We are not living from the basis of our results, but we are living from the basis of his results. We are not living based on our status, but we are living based on his status. Jesus took my sin, sickness, and disease without earning it and died in my place so that I could receive his righteousness, health, and prosperity without earning it. I get it by his grace and by believing.

God says this is his wisdom by prescription. This is how you, the new creation in the world partake—"as he is". God says I am giving wisdom as to how to partake of how he is. The bread is how in the world we partake of how 'he is'. The cup is how you in this world partake of him as he is. God is literally saying to us that this is how the new creation downloads the results of the finished work of Jesus of Nazareth. This is one of the ways that his righteousness, healing, health soundness, and prosperity are transmitted to you and me in this world.

For years, the enemy has set the stage to hit the whole wide world with coronavirus pandemic, and now it has hit the nations of the earth. It took the powers of darkness years to set a catastrophe. It took the corporation of men and demons years to set evil ambushes for destruction on earth. The enemy has for years been setting a stage on which he could release death and fear internationally without a physical war.

Three generations ago, he did it through World War I. Two generations ago, he did it with World War II. Now the world has convinced all these entities to keep us from going to global war, but they don't have an answer for this and for other pandemics yet to come because the enemy has been planning for another way. **However, the new creation has the answer**.

In all these, God says that this is "my wisdom for you"—the communion. He tells us, "I have given my wisdom to you, new creation, to get a transfusion of his blood where the health, wealth, soundness, and righteousness that Jesus has accomplished on your behalf can actually be transmitted to you through the communion if you will rightly discern the Lord's day. Apostle Paul tells us in 1 Corinthians 11 that when many partake of the Lord's communion, they may leave there weak, sick, and dying for they fail to rightly discern the Lord's body. They do not pass the ritual to revelation.

Please understand by the way of revelation that when you and I take that bread and that cup, there is a special substance transfusion of who Jesus is into your spirit, soul, and body. The question I keep hearing God asking is "Whose wisdom and whose report will you believe?" I submit to you today, if you are trusting in the blood and the body of Jesus understanding that on the cross, that body became sin and took your sickness and disease, the coronavirus was already laid on Jesus on the calvary. If they find another disease next year, that too was laid on Jesus' body. And if five years from now there is another one, then he already took that one too. Therefore, if you receive the body that bore the virus in your place and receive it as yours, it is accounted to you. God has it recorded that you already had the coronavirus and been recovered from it.

In the wisdom of God, he has it recorded that the coronavirus has already hit you and that you have recovered from it. It is now separated from you and you have been separated from it. That is the record in heaven. Whose report do you believe? God has it recorded that you have already risen with the body that cannot be touched with the coronavirus or any other. Whose report will you believe? As often as you do this, you proclaim, and declare it cannot touch you.

You may be asking, "How can that be, author?" Well, that is grace; you didn't earn it. Now your healing does not come by avoidance, but by your participation in the work that Jesus finished on your behalf. I encourage you to partake of the Lord's table for your healing, deliverance, protection, and provision that Jesus redeemed to give you. It is yours for participating in the Lord's communion.

CHAPTER 13

Taking Lord's Communion

1 Corinthians 11:23–34—"²³ For I received from the Lord Himself that [instruction] which I passed on to you, that the Lord Jesus on the night in which He was betrayed took bread; ²⁴ and when He had given thanks, He broke it and said, "This is (represents) My body, which is [offered as a sacrifice] for you. Do this in [affectionate] remembrance of Me." ²⁵ In the same way, after supper He took the cup, saying, "This cup is the new covenant [ratified and established] in My blood; do this, as often as you drink it, in [affectionate] remembrance of Me." ²⁶ For every time you eat this bread and drink this cup, you are [symbolically] proclaiming [the fact of] the Lord's death until He comes [again].

²⁷ So then whoever eats the bread or drinks the cup of the Lord in a way that is unworthy [of Him] will be guilty of [profaning and sinning against] the body and blood of the Lord. ²⁸ But a person must [prayerfully] examine himself [and his relationship to Christ], and only when he has done so should he eat of the bread and drink of the cup. ²⁹ For anyone who eats and drinks [without solemn reverence and heartfelt gratitude for the sacrifice of Christ], eats and drinks a judgment on himself if he does not [¡]recognize the body [of Christ]. ³⁰ That [careless and unworthy participation] is the reason why

many among you are weak and sick, and a number sleep [in death]. ³¹ But if we evaluated and judged ourselves honestly [recognizing our shortcomings and correcting our behavior], we would not be judged. ³² But when we [fall short and] are judged by the Lord, we are disciplined [by undergoing His correction] so that we will not be condemned [to eternal punishment] along with the world.

³³ So then, my brothers and sisters, when you come together to eat [the Lord's Supper], wait for one another [and see to it that no one is left out]. ³⁴ If anyone is too hungry [to wait], let him eat at home, so that you will not come together for judgment [on yourselves]."

Reverently, please follow through with instructions I am giving for proper participation of the Lord's table. Please take your emblems (bread and the cup) in your hands and participate in the Lord's table. You can do this by yourself, family, couple, or at your house church.

1. If the coronavirus has not touched you, it will not.
2. If it has touched you or somebody else you know, I declare in the name of Jesus that at this moment, your recovery begins.
3. I declare to you that you will not have chills or temperatures of 101°F and above.
4. You will have no symptoms of coronavirus.
5. You are coming out as nothing has touched you.
6. I declare it is possible for you to recover starting now.
7. By the spirit of God, what takes 14, 21 days, or a month for others is going to take less than 24 hours for you.
8. Those dealing with symptoms right now, by the close of the day, the symptoms will have left you.
9. Fear is no match to the anointing.
10. All you have to do now is to receive it.
11. I got faith in you. Just connect with mine.
12. Now take the bread in your hand and say out loud with me.

a. Lord, as I take the bread, I am trusting you.
b. I am exercising the wisdom that comes from above.
c. I decide today I will trust the wisdom of God.
d. Lord, you have given communion as a part of your wisdom so that the finished work of Jesus in the heavens can be transmitted, transfused, and transferred to the rest of your body in the earth.
e. I am a part of that body and what is true of the head is true of the body.
f. He is righteous.
    i. I am righteous.
g. He is healed, well, and recovered.
    i. I am healed, well, and recovered.
h. He has no lack and no needs unmet.
    i. I have no lack and no needs unmet.
i. I declare now he took my sin, sickness, including the coronavirus.
j. He took my poverty.
k. I receive that body as my own.
l. And I declare heaven has it recorded.
    i. I have already died and risen, free from every disease.
m. In the name of Jesus;
    i. Let us eat all together.
    ii. Say Lord, I receive that.

13. Now take the cup in your hand.
    a. Jesus said this cup is the new covenant (agreement) in my blood.
    b. When you drink it, you are drinking in the agreement.
    c. When you drink it, you are declaring before God, the angels, and the demons that you believe in the agreement that what Jesus did belongs to you.

- d. He did it without earning it, so I can have the results without earning them.
- e. So, Jesus said this is the new agreement—that there is a transfusion of life flowing out of you into your blood, lungs, and respiratory system.
- f. The life of God is flowing out of his spirit into your spirit and physical body.
- g. Lift the cup and say:
    - i. Lord Jesus as I drink this cup,
    - ii. I am trusting in your wisdom that comes from above.
    - iii. This is the new agreement that it is not my performance that merits your goodness;
    - iv. But it is by trusting in the finished work of Jesus on my behalf.
    - v. I am righteous, healed, provided for.
    - vi. In Jesus' name, Amen.
    - vii. Let us all drink together. Hallelujah…
    - viii. Lift up your hands and thank God for the finished work of Jesus at the cross, at the calvary.

SONG: 1. Burdens are lifted at calvary, calvary, calvary
            2. Jesus there is something about your name

CHAPTER 14

Right Standing with God

In these uncertain times, regardless of the mistakes we made and the sin we committed in the past, this would be an appropriate time to consider coming to right standing with God and receiving abundant life which includes salvation and healing of your spirit, soul, and body. God is asking you a question in Luke 9:25, "... .What profit is it to a man if he gains the whole world, and he himself is destroyed or lost?" COVID-19 is a pestilence and a sign of the end of the age. In Matthew 24:4-8, Jesus said to his disciples:

> "Take heed that no one deceives you. ⁵ For many will come in My name, saying, 'I am the Christ,' and will deceive many. ⁶ And you will hear of wars and rumors of wars. See that you are not troubled; for all these things must come to pass, but the end is not yet. ⁷ For nation will rise against nation, and kingdom against kingdom. And there will be famines, pestilences, and earthquakes in various places. ⁸ All these are the beginning of sorrows."

God has provided a way out of these predicaments. In the Bible, 1 John 1:9 reads, "If we confess our sins, He is faithful and just to forgive us our sins and to cleanse us from all unrighteousness."

This is why Jesus died for us at the cross. Although he never sinned, he became sin so we could become righteous by dying for us at the cross. The great news of the gospel is that Jesus Christ never changes. He was the healer then as he is still the healer now. He was the forgiver then and he is still as forgiving today. He was the savior then and he is still saving today. It is written in the Bible in 1 John 4:14, "And we have seen and testify that the Father has sent the Son as Savior of the world." Jesus is ready to save you now so you can be accounted as an heir of the kingdom of heaven. He will completely wash and cleanse you from all unrighteousness. He will take away every torment, set you free indeed, and give you peace that passes all understanding. All you have to do is to repent and receive forgiveness by muttering what he said about you in Romans 10:9, "that if you confess with your mouth the Lord Jesus and believe in your heart that God has raised Him from the dead, you will be saved."

Prayer for Salvation

Please repeat this prayer after me purposing in your heart to be saved:

Father, I receive your gift of eternal life in the person of Jesus Christ according to your word recorded in Romans 6:23, "That the wages of sin is **death, but the gift of God** is **eternal life in Christ Jesus our** Lord." I repent of my deeds and ask you to forgive me. I receive you into my heart. Come in me and make your home with me. I forgive everyone who have ought against or hurt me. I release them to your word and mercy. I confess Jesus is Lord of my life from today. I believe you raised him from the dead. He lives forevermore and now he is alive in me. I declare I am saved to the uttermost. In Jesus' name. Amen.

What has happened

Now you have become a child of God by the reason of forgiveness of sin and washing by the blood of Jesus. You are a new creation; your former life has passed away and all has become new. You can function the way God functions. You have his character, nature, and authority. You are precious to him and he is very protective of you. In Zechariah 2:8 it says, "…. he who touches you touches the apple of His eye".

In 1 Peter 2:9–10, it says, "you are a chosen generation, a royal priesthood, a holy nation, His own special people, that may proclaim the praises of Him who called you out of darkness into His marvelous light; ¹⁰ who once were not a people but are now the people of God, who had not obtained mercy but now have obtained mercy."

In John 15:7, Jesus told us, "If you abide in Me, and My words abide in you, you will ask what you desire, and it shall be done for you." Now you have the right to ask for the hedge of protection from COVID-19 and from all other pestilences, sickness, and disease.

CHAPTER 15

Hedge of Protection Prayer

Overcoming and breaking the spirit of fear is key to a victorious life in Christ Jesus.

> Job 1:10—"Have You not put a hedge [of protection] around him and his house and all that he has, on every side? You have blessed the work of his hands [and conferred prosperity and happiness upon him], and his possessions have increased in the land."

No evil power or devil can penetrate the divine hedge of protection that God has put around the new creation. It is very clear in this text that Satan had no power over Job, not until God himself removed the hedge. The divine hedge keeps the enemy out

A hedge is a wall or fence built around a precious property or possession to prevent damage or theft. My wife and I have built a fence around our poultry business for both biosecurity, damage, and theft prevention. A hedge is usually set up for the purpose of protection or defense. In the above text, all believers (the new creation) were likened to a vineyard with the precious vine. Just as God fenced the vineyard, he surrounds every believer with a divine hedge as in Psalm 91:1-2—"He who dwells in the secret place of the Most High Shall abide under the shadow of the Almighty. ²I will say of the LORD, "He is my refuge and my fortress, my God, in Him I will trust".

Facts about the Divine Hedge

First, the divine hedge is God himself.

Psalm 125:1-2—"Those who trust in the LORD are like Mount Zion, which cannot be moved, but abides forever. ²As the mountains surround Jerusalem, so the LORD surrounds His people from this time forth and forever."

During any battle, the people of Israel locate the mountains as a weapon of defense, and just as the mountains surround Jerusalem, so the Lord himself surrounds the new creation.

Second, the divine hedge is also known as the "wall of fire".

Zechariah 2:5—"Our God is a consuming fire and because of His love for us, He protects us with a wall of fire."

Third, the divine hedge is invisible.

2 Kings 6:17—"¹⁷And Elisha prayed, and said, "LORD, I pray, open his eyes that he may see." Then the LORD opened the eyes of the young man, and he saw. And behold, the mountain was full of horses and chariots of fire all around Elisha."

The divine hedge is so real, yet it is invisible. Elisha had to pray to God to open the eyes of Gehazi, so he could see the mighty army. If God could protect his servant in this manner, how much more the children of the Most High.

Fourth, no evil power or devil can penetrate the divine hedge.

Job 1:10—"Have You not made a hedge around him, around his household, and around all that he has on every side? You have blessed the work of his hands, and his possessions have increased in the land."

It is very clear in this text that Satan had no power over Job, not until God himself removed the hedge.

Fifth, the divine hedge keeps the enemy out.

Sixth, the divine hedge comes with commandments.

Ecclesiastes 10:8—"He who digs a pit will fall into it, and whoever breaks through a wall will be bitten by a serpent."

Whenever God creates a vineyard as he did in the garden of Eden, he will always give instructions else the haven or refuge is lost just like the beginning. So, God does not expect us as believers to break the hedge by our disobedience.

Seventh, the divine hedge could be broken or removed.

Isaiah 5:5—"And now, please let Me tell you what I will do to My vineyard. I will take away its hedge, and it shall be burned, and break down its wall, and it shall be trampled down."

Jesus told us that we did not choose him, but he chose us and appointed us that we should go and bear fruit, and *that* our fruit should remain; that whatever we ask the Father in his name, he may give us.

God expects so much from us because he has invested so much in us, and so it pains him to see unproductive Christians. Sometimes, he may have no choice but to remove the hedge as a consequence of unfruitfulness.

God's Reasons for Removing the Hedge

First is ignoring God's directives.

Joshua 7:1—"But the children of Israel committed a trespass regarding the accursed things, for Achan the son of Carmi, the son of Zabdi, the son of Zerah, of the tribe of Judah, took of the accursed thing, so the anger of the LORD burned against the children of Israel."

Joshua and all the Israelites had just won a battle against the city of Jericho but due to their disobedience on the instructions of the Lord, they lost to a small country—Ai. Failure to comply with God's directives always tend to draw people out of God's presence, and the hedge will be removed by God.

Second is unfruitfulness.

Isaiah 5:4–5—"What more could have been done to My vineyard that I have not done in it? Why then, when I expected it to bring forth good grapes, did it bring forth wild grapes? ⁵ And now, please let Me tell you what I will do to My vineyard: I will take away its hedge, and it shall be burned, and break down its wall, and it shall be trampled down."

God hates unfruitfulness. When Jesus got to the fig tree and he could not find fruit on it, he cursed it. So, if as a Christian, God has deposited a gift or talent in you and you refused to utilize it for the glory of God, then God may decide to remove the hedge just as he did in this text.

Third is trials.

God allows trials or temptations to come. It's important to note that trials will surely come but what we do during trials is what's very important. Hence, God could remove the hedge just to see how much you love him.

Other reasons include rebelling against God's anointed, prayerlessness, carelessness, and going against God's will.

Signs of a Broken Hedge

Consider what Job suffered as a result of God's removal of the divine hedge.

> Job 1:13–22—"Now there was a day when his sons and daughters were eating and drinking wine in their oldest brother's house, [14] and a messenger came to Job and said, "The oxen were plowing and the donkeys feeding beside them, [15] when the Sabean raided them and took them away—indeed they have killed the servants with the edge of the sword; and I alone have escaped to tell you!" [16] While he was still speaking, another also came and said, "The fire of God fell from heaven and burned up the sheep and the servants, and [c]consumed them; and I alone have escaped to tell you!" [17] While he was still speaking, another also came and said, "The Chaldeans formed three bands, raided the camels and took them away, yes, and killed the servants with the edge of the sword; and I alone have escaped to tell you!" [18] While he

was still speaking, another also came and said, "Your sons and daughters were eating and drinking wine in their oldest brother's house, [19] and suddenly a great wind came from [d]across the wilderness and struck the four corners of the house, and it fell on the young people, and they are dead; and I alone have escaped to tell you!" [20] Then Job arose, tore his robe, and shaved his head; and he fell to the ground and worshiped. [21] And he said "Naked I came from my mother's womb, and naked shall I return there. The LORD gave, and the LORD has taken away. Blessed be the name of the LORD." [22] In all this Job did not sin nor charge God with wrong."

We can see the evidence of a broken or removed hedge. What you expect from a broken or removed hedge is the affliction by the enemy on yourself or any member of the family through poverty, great loss, disaster, sickness, glory turning to shame as in the case of Samson, and sin taking dominion over you or them.

How to Rebuild a Broken Hedge

If a builder discovers a broken wall, he knows that trying to patch it will not bring a lasting solution. Instead, he breaks down that section of the wall and rebuilds it from the very foundation. Hence, if the divine hedge must be rebuilt, the foundation must be revisited. The following actions will help in building and strengthening the divine hedge of all the new creation:

Repentance—God will only protect his own.

2 Chronicles 7:14—"If My people who are called by My name will humble themselves, and pray and seek My face, and turn from their wicked ways, then I will hear from heaven, and will forgive their sin and heal their land."

Praying is the best form of defense from attack. You do this by putting on the whole armor of God.

Ephesians 6:11—"Put on the whole armor of God, that you may be able to stand against the [a]wiles of the devil."

Offer quality offering unto the Lord, pleading the blood of Jesus Christ. During the Passover night, the blood of the Lamb formed the hedge for the children of Israel, and it is still so at this age—the blood of Jesus forms the hedge for us, the sons of God.

Seeking God's anointing restores the broken hedge.

Psalm 105:14–15 —"He permitted no one to do them wrong; Yes, He rebuked kings for their sakes[15] saying, "Do not touch My anointed ones, and do My prophets no harm."

Living a holy life and staying in God's presence always through worship will rebuild the broken hedge.

Psalm 91:1—"He who dwells in the secret place of the Most High Shall abide under the shadow of the Almighty."

Declaration:

Jeremiah 33:3—Father I call to You, and You answer me, and show me great and mighty things, which I do not know.

Psalm 50:15—Lord, I call upon you in this time of COVID-19 trouble. You deliver me, and I glorify You.

Psalm 59:16— I sing of Your power. Yes, I sing aloud of Your mercy in the morning for You are my defense and refuge in the day of trouble.

Psalm 77:2—In the day of my trouble I sought the Lord; my hand was stretched out in the night without ceasing; my soul refused to be comforted.

Psalm 86:7—In the day of my trouble, I will call upon You, for You will answer me.

Psalm 102:2—Do not hide Your face from me in the day of my trouble; incline Your ear to me; in the day that I call, answer me speedily.

Breaking the Spirit of Fear

Psalm 27:1—LORD you are my light and my salvation and I'm not fearful. You are the strength of my life." I'm not afraid of coronavirus pandemic.

Joel 2:21—I fear not, I am glad and rejoice, for you LORD has done marvelous things before my eyes.

Hebrews 13:6—I boldly confess You are my helper; I will not fear. What can coronavirus pandemic do to me?

2 Corinthians 12:9—Lord I declare that Your grace is sufficient for me to deal with coronavirus pandemic, for your power is perfected in weakness. I boast about my weaknesses, so that the power of Christ may dwell in me."

Zechariah 4:6—For it is not by might nor by power, but by Your Spirit Lord Almighty, that coronavirus pandemic is removed. Lord, preserve me and your redeemed in the earth.

2 Samuel 22:3—My God, my rock, in You I take refuge, my shield and the horn of my salvation, my stronghold and my refuge. My savior, You save me from violent pestilences and coronavirus pandemic.

Psalm 18:2—LORD You are my rock and my fortress and my deliverer. My God, my rock, in You I take refuge, my shield and the horn of my salvation, my stronghold.

Isaiah 59:19— Satan, hear me and hear me clearly—although you have come in like a flood in the form of a coronavirus pandemic, the Spirit of the Lord raises and lifts up a standard against you. Yes, you may have blown strong winds of pandemics, but I and the children God has given me are like that house built on a Rock, unmoved and unshaken.

Preserve me, Lord, for your name's sake. Wherever the fearful and unbelieving may fall, Lord, I pray that I may stand in the name of Jesus. You are my rock, you are my refuge, you are my hiding place.

Psalm 94:22—Lord you are my defense and the rock of my refuge.

Father, as I enter into every new day, may the womb of my morning open, and may it bring forth an abundance of blessings and favor. Lord, whatever my hands will touch, may it be fruitful, and may it prosper in the name of Jesus.

Lord, I pray for protection in the name of Jesus. I pray that you go before me in my going out and in my coming in, in the name of Jesus.

I pray and declare that the sun shall not smite me by day nor the moon by night, for you are my light and my salvation. Lead me, guide me, and order my steps in safety, as it is written in Psalm 37:23, "The steps of a righteous man are ordered by the Lord, and He delights in his way."

Lord, may you cover me and my loved ones under the shadow of your wings. May you assign your angels to take charge over me to protect me in the name of Jesus Christ.

Lord, I pray may you set a wall of fire around me and my family, and may the plans of the enemy be turned upside down.

In Isaiah 54:17, I declare and decree in the name of Jesus Christ that "No weapon formed against me shall prosper, and I condemn every tongue which rises against me in judgment. This is my heritage as Your servant, and my righteousness is from You," in the name of Jesus. Lord, I thank you for answering my prayer. I testify you are good and your mercies endure forever.

Our God is the good shepherd and he has provided divine protection and defense for his new creation. However, it is the responsibility of the new creation to ensure that this hedge is not broken by speaking his word on earth as he has spoken on earth. If you are still out of the fold, this is the time to come into safety. Please repent now.

Safety of Abiding in God's Presence (Psalm 91)

Now declare and decree with me and David protection over our lives and our descendants against perilous pestilences, including COVID-19.

> Father, I declare You are the Almighty and the Most High, and above You, there is no other God. I declare I dwell in Your secret place and therefore, I abide under Your shadow where the devil can do me no harm.
> I say of You LORD, You are my refuge and my fortress, my God, in You I trust.
> Surely, You deliver me from the snare of the fowler and from the perilous pestilence.
> You cover me with Your feathers, and under Your wings, I take refuge. Your truth is my shield and buckler.
> I am not afraid of the terror by night, nor of the arrow that flies by day, nor of the pestilence that walks in darkness, nor of the destruction that lays waste at noonday.
> A thousand may fall at my side, and ten thousand at my right hand; but it does not come near me.
> Only with my eyes do I look and see the reward of the wicked.
> Because I have made the LORD, who is my refuge, even the Most High, my dwelling place, no evil shall befall me, nor shall any plague come near my dwelling.
> For You give Your angels charge over me to keep me in all my ways. In their hands they bear me up, lest I dash my foot against a stone.

I tread upon the lion and the cobra; the young lion and the serpent I trample all underfoot.

Lord, You deliver me because I have set my love upon You.

Lord, You set me on high, because I have known Your name. I call upon You, and You answer me.

Lord, You are with me in trouble. You deliver me and honor me. With long life, You satisfy and show me Your salvation.

I count it done in the name of Jesus Christ. Amen.

CHAPTER 16

Prayers of Faith

Praying for Nations

Luke 2:30–32—Father, we declare Jesus is our salvation. We acknowledge and receive him as the God-revealing light to the non-Jewish nations and the light of glory for your people Israel.

Psalms 2:8—We ask you to give us the nations for an inheritance and the ends of the earth for our possession.

Psalms 72:11—All kings shall fall down before you. All nations shall serve you. In the name of Jesus, we bring before you the nation of Israel, United States, United Kingdom, Kenya, and other nations of the earth and their leaders; and decree they fall down before you to worship.

Psalm 105:14—Father, we thank you for not permitting no one to do our leaders wrong; yes, we ask you to rebuke leaders for our sake as in 1 Timothy 2:1–2, so that we may live a quiet and peaceable life in all godliness and honesty.

Proverbs 2:10–15; 28:2—We pray that skillful and godly wisdom will enter the hearts of Israel's, United States', United Kingdom's, Kenya's and other nations' leaders; and that knowledge shall be pleasant to them, that discretion will watch over them, and that understanding will keep them and deliver them from the way of evil and from the evil men; that the right will be prolonged.

Proverbs 2:21–22—We pray that the upright shall dwell in the governments, that men and women of integrity, blameless and complete in your sight shall remain, but the wicked shall be cut off and the treacherous shall be rooted out.

Proverbs 20:26, 28—We pray that those in authority winnow (get rid of) the wicked from among the good and bring the threshing wheel over them to separate the chaff from the grain for loving kindness, mercy, truth, and faithfulness preserve those in authority, and their offices are upheld by the peoples' loyalty.

Proverbs 16:10, 12–13—Father, we declare that our leaders do not commit wickedness and their leadership is established by righteousness. Father, we ask you to direct the decisions made by these leaders, and that present leaders who are men and women of discretion, understanding, and knowledge will remain in the office so the stability of Israel, United States, United Kingdom, Kenya, and other nations will long continue.

Proverbs 29:2—We pray that the uncompromisingly righteous will be in authority in Israel, United States, United Kingdom, Kenya, and other nations so the people can rejoice.

Proverbs 21:1—We decree the hearts of our leaders are in your hand, and like the rivers of water, you turn them wherever you wish.

Psalm 68:11—We pray that their offices be established and made secure by righteousness; and that right and just lips are a delight to those in authority; and that they love those who speak what is right.

Acts 12:24—We pray and believe that the good news of the gospel is published in the land.

We thank you for the laborers of the harvest to publish your word that Jesus is Lord in Israel, United States, United Kingdom, Kenya, and other nations of the earth.

We thank you for raising up intercessors to pray for the nations of the earth. In Jesus' name, Amen

American Government

1 Timothy 2:1-3—Father, in the name of Jesus, we thank you for the United States and its government. We hold up in prayer before you those in positions of authority. We pray and intercede for the president, the representatives, the senators, the judges of our land, governors, mayors, and for all those in authority over us in any way, as well as the armed forces and police force. We pray that the spirit of the Lord rests upon them.

Proverbs 21:10–12—We believe that skillful and godly wisdom has entered into the heart of our president and that knowledge be pleasant to him. Discretion watches over him. Knowledge keeps him and delivers him from the way of evil and from evil men.

Proverbs 2:21-22—Father, we ask you to compass the president with men and women who make their hearts and ears attentive to godly counsel and do that which is right in your sight. We believe you cause them to be men and women of integrity who are obedient concerning us that we may lead a quiet and peaceable life in all godliness and honesty. We pray that the upright shall dwell in our government.

May men and women who are blameless and complete in your sight remain in these positions of authority, but the wicked be cut off from our government and the treacherous shall be rooted out of it.

Psalm 33:12—Father, your word declares that "Blessed is the nation whose God is their Lord". We receive your blessing.

2 Samuel 22:3—Father, you are the God of our strength, in whom we trust; our shield and the horn of our salvation; our stronghold and our refuge. Our Savior, you save us from violence.

Deuteronomy 28:10–11—Father, we declare all peoples of America are called by the name of the LORD, and that they revere you. You, LORD, **grant** us plenty of goods, in the fruit of your body, in the increase of your livestock, and in the produce of your ground, in the land of which you LORD have given us. Father, you are our refuge and stronghold in times of troubles (high cost, destitution, and desperation). So, we declare with our mouth that your people dwell safely in this land, and we prosper abundantly.

Proverbs 1:33—We decree American leaders listen to godly counsel and make heavenly decisions that make us dwell safely, secure, and without fear of evil.

Proverbs 9:9—The leaders of our nation are wise. They receive your instruction and become still wiser.

They are just leaders and let the Holy Spirit teach them and increase their learning.

Proverbs 21:1—Father, you have said in your word that the heart of the king is in the hand of the Lord and you turn it whichever way you desire. We believe the hearts of our leaders are in your hand and that their decisions are divinely directed by the Lord.

Acts 12:24—Thank you, Lord, because the good news of the gospel is published in our land. Thank you, Lord, because your word prevails and grows mightily in the hearts and lives of the people. Thank you for this land and the leaders you have given to us. In the name of Jesus of Nazareth. Jesus, you are Lord over United States of America!

Father, bless the United States of America! Amen.

The Nation and People of Israel

Psalms 94:14—Lord, we acknowledge that you do not cast off nor spurn your people, neither will you abandon your heritage.

Psalm 74:20—Father, you have regard for the covenant which you made with Abraham.

Leviticus 26:42—Father, remember your covenant with Abraham, Isaac, and Jacob and remember the land to fulfill it.

Psalms 122:6-9—Father, we pray for the peace of Jerusalem. Those who love your holy city are prospered. We proclaim peace be within their walls and prosperity within their palaces for their brethren and companions' sakes. We now say, "Peace be within you, Israel". For the sake of your house, Lord our God, we seek, inquire for, and require your good.

Ephesians 2:14—Thank you, Father, for bringing the people of Israel into unity with one another and for bringing your church both Jews and Gentiles into oneness—as one new man—and breaking down the barrier and the dividing wall of spiritual antagonism between us.

Thank you, Lord, for the peace treaties with Israel's former enemies. We decree these treaties are used for good to make way for the good news of the gospel as we prepare for the coming of our Messiah.

Romans 11:7, 11—We intercede for those who have become callously indifferent, blinded, hardened, and made insensitive to the gospel. We pray that they will not fall to their utter spiritual ruin. It was through their false step and transgression that salvation has come to the gentiles.

Ephesians 1:18—Now, we ask for the eyes of their understanding to be enlightened that they may know the Messiah who is to make himself known to all of Israel.

Zachariah 10:6,12—Lord, we ask you to strengthen the house of Judah and save the house of Joseph. Thank you, Father for restoring them because you have compassion on them. We say, they are strong as though you had not rejected them, for you are the Lord their God, and you answer them. Thank you, Lord, for your great mercy and love for them and for us, in the name of Jesus our Messiah.

Psalm 106:47-48—Thank you, Father, for saving Israel and gathering them from nations, that they may give thanks to your holy name and glory in your praise. Praise be to you, Lord, the God of Israel, everlasting to everlasting; and all the people say, Amen!

We praise you Lord for blessing the nation and people of Israel. In Jesus' name. Amen!

Peace of Jerusalem

Psalms 122:6—Father, according to your Word, we acknowledge, love, and pray for the peace of Jerusalem, that the inhabitants may be born again. We pray that you, Lord, are the refuge and a stronghold to the children of Israel. We receive the prosperity that comes with loving Israel and praying for the peace of Jerusalem.

Joel 3:14—Father, your word says, "multitudes are in the valley of decision" and whoever calls upon your name shall be delivered and saved.

Job 22:30—Have mercy upon Israel and be gracious to them, O Lord, and consider that they fight for their land to be restored. You, Lord, are their strength and stronghold in their day of trouble. We pray that they are righteous before you and that you will make even their enemies be at peace with them. Your word says that you will deliver those for whom we intercede, who are not innocent, through the cleanness of our hands. May they realize that their defense and shield depend on you.

Thank you, Lord, for your word that you have a covenant with Israel and that you have taken away their sin. They are your beloved.

Lord, your word in Romans 11:29 also says that your gifts are irrevocable, that you never withdraw them once they are given, and that you do not change your mind about those to whom you give your grace or to whom you send your call.

Isaiah 45:17—Though they have been disobedient and rebellious toward you, Lord, we pray that now they repent and obtain your mercy and forgiveness through your son, Jesus. We praise you, Lord for your compassion and forgiveness to your people. We praise you that they are under your protection and divine guidance, that they are your special possession, your peculiar treasure, and that you spare them because we have read in word that all Israel shall be saved. You shall not be ashamed or disgraced forever and ever.

Father, I commit to pray for the peace of Jerusalem! Thank you, Father, for delivering us all from every evil work and for the authority you have given us with the name of Jesus. We love you and praise you. Every day, with its new reasons, we praise you.

I pray for the peace of Jerusalem. I am prospering because I love you "the holy city!" Peace is within my walls and prosperity within my palaces! Amen.

Declaration:

Father, I declare my best days are with me. I speak blessing and favor into my tomorrow. I speak a hundredfold increase—one thousand more numerous times multiplication and replenishment. Lord, you delight in the prosperity of your servant. I speak prosperity into my weekend, my next week, my next month, the years to come, and my future. I decree that favor meet me tomorrow. Lord, I declare you surround me with faithful men and women—trustworthy friends who will encourage my faith and strengthen me in the things of God.

Thank you, Lord, for giving me favor in the sight of my culprits who denied, intercepted, and interrupted my receiving, so now they have granted me *what I request*. Thus, I have plundered them.

I decree the wealth of the sinner, which was stored up for me. I meet it in my immediate future.

I declare my heart is swollen with joy because the abundance of the sea has been turned to me. The wealth of the Gentiles has come to me.

My gates are open continually. They are never shut day or night that *men* bring to me the wealth of the Gentiles and their kings in procession.